# Bach's *Art of Fugue* and *Musical Offering*

# ABS GUIDES

*Series Editor*
Steven Zohn

*Bach's Art of Fugue and Musical Offering*
**Matthew Dirst**

# Bach's *Art of Fugue* and *Musical Offering*

MATTHEW DIRST

OXFORD
UNIVERSITY PRESS

# OXFORD
### UNIVERSITY PRESS

Oxford University Press is a department of the University of Oxford. It furthers
the University's objective of excellence in research, scholarship, and education
by publishing worldwide. Oxford is a registered trade mark of Oxford University
Press in the UK and certain other countries.

Published in the United States of America by Oxford University Press
198 Madison Avenue, New York, NY 10016, United States of America.

© Oxford University Press 2024

Library of Congress Cataloging-in-Publication Data
Names: Dirst, Matthew, author.
Title: Bach's Art of fugue and Musical offering / Matthew Dirst.
Description: New York, NY : Oxford University Press, 2024. |
Series: ABS guides |
Includes bibliographical references and index.
Identifiers: LCCN 2023017609 (print) | LCCN 2023017610 (ebook) |
ISBN 9780197536643 (paperback) | ISBN 9780197536636 (hardback) |
ISBN 9780197536667 (epub) | ISBN 9780197536674
Subjects: LCSH: Bach, Johann Sebastian, 1685–1750—Criticism and interpretation. |
Bach, Johann Sebastian, 1685-1750. Kunst der Fuge. | Bach, Johann Sebastian, 1685–1750.
Musikalisches Opfer. | Fugue. | Music—18th century—History and criticism.
Classification: LCC ML410.B13 D587 2023 (print) |
LCC ML410.B13 (ebook) | DDC 784.18/72—dc23/eng/20230519
LC record available at https://lccn.loc.gov/2023017609
LC ebook record available at https://lccn.loc.gov/2023017610

DOI: 10.1093/oso/9780197536636.001.0001

Paperback printed by Marquis Book Printing, Canada
Hardback printed by Bridgeport National Bindery, Inc., United States of America

# Contents

Sponsored by the
**RUTH AND NOEL MONTE FUND OF
THE AMERICAN BACH SOCIETY**

*Ruth and Noel Monte were deeply devoted to
Bach and his music, sensing its great impact
on the human brain and culture throughout
the world. To them, Bach represented a bright
planet appearing in the sky only once, requiring
centuries for the human mind to observe and
fully comprehend. The Monte Fund has the goal
of supporting and promoting this living musical
treasure for present and future generations.*

# Series Editor's Foreword

Few composers of any time or place have inspired as many words as Johann Sebastian Bach. For well over two centuries, generations of writers have contributed to a now voluminous literature on the composer's life and works. Yet because a large portion of this literature approaches the music from a highly technical perspective, Bach enthusiasts who lack extensive musical training find themselves looking in from the outside, as it were. More accessible writings often avoid discussing the music itself, which is of course what draws listeners to Bach in the first place; instead, they tend to limit themselves to investigating Bach's biography, the social contexts for music-making in his time, or the theological interpretation of his sacred vocal works. Non-specialist literature that does focus on the music often perpetuates myths or engages in misguided (if well-meaning) attempts to reveal supposed compositional secrets.

The present volume, as with others in this series of guides sponsored by the American Bach Society, is by an expert in the field who aims to offer a lucid, engaging, and timely exploration of Bach's music for a broad audience. Central to this exploration is the experience of listening to Bach's music in his time and ours. Attention is also devoted to the music's genesis, history, organization, meaning, and contexts, this last category encompassing perspectives that may be musical, biographical, social, political, performance-practical, and theological. Authors assume no technical knowledge about music on the reader's part, and although musical examples make occasional appearances, they are intended to be illustrative of the discussion rather than integral to it. Finally, the brief suggestions for further reading that follow each chapter and the selective bibliography at the end of the volume emphasize literature in English.

Among the many people who have made this series possible, special thanks are due to my predecessor Daniel R. Melamed, without whose vision and advocacy it could never have materialized, and to Norman Hirschy and Rada Radojicic at Oxford University Press, whose enthusiasm and support for the project have been essential to its realization.

Steven Zohn
General Editor, American Bach Society

# Acknowledgments

As the author of the initial volume in a new series produced jointly by the American Bach Society and Oxford University Press, I would like to acknowledge both organizations and thank them for the opportunity to write about two such fascinating musical works. My initial plan for this study was to fill a longstanding gap in the general literature on the *Art of Fugue* and *Musical Offering* while synthesizing a wealth of specialist writing on these late exemplars of Bach's contrapuntal art. That brief expanded somewhat as I took account of the idiosyncrasies of individual pieces and wide-ranging responses to both collections in various media, from musical scholarship to visual art and literature. On virtually all topics covered in the following pages, I am indebted to a community of writers and artists for insight into this extraordinary music and its eternal allure.

A 2019/20 Faculty Development Leave from the University of Houston provided a crucial jump-start for this project during a year like few others, when working at home suddenly became the norm. Hearty thanks to Suzanne Ryan Melamed, Mary Horn, Norman Hirschy, and Rada Radojicic, who have all been supportive shepherds of the series and this volume at OUP, and to Daniel R. Melamed, ABS President and former General Editor, who offered perceptive advice at the proposal stage. Steven Zohn, ABS General Editor, graciously provided detailed commentary on the entire manuscript, and Ryan Rogers set with exemplary skill and professionalism all musical examples. I am also grateful to an outside reader whose feedback caused me to reframe certain sections of the book and to rework various passages. The completion of this volume owes much, finally, to my husband Sixto Wagan, whose good humor, steadfast companionship, and digital expertise enabled steady progress on it despite the manifold disruptions of a pandemic. Thankfully, research and writing in the arts and humanities are mostly solitary activities, and Bach's music, as always, provided plenty of inspiration and food for thought.

Matthew Dirst

# Introduction

The music of Johann Sebastian Bach has long been central to multiple constituencies, each of which tends to favor a different part of his output. Virtually all professional orchestras—whether period or modern instrument—trot out the "Brandenburg" Concertos and the "Orchestral" Suites for eager audiences, while keyboard players of all stripes treat the *Well-Tempered Clavier* (*WTC*) with a respect bordering on veneration. Other works from this composer have inspired niche markets of their own, with cantatas and passion settings keeping choirs great and small happily occupied and unaccompanied works for violin, cello, and flute providing ideal fare for the lone virtuoso. This book takes up two iconic and closely related collections treasured by specialists but known in the greater musical community more by reputation than firm acquaintance. Bach's *Art of Fugue* and *Musical Offering*—both grounded in tradition yet utterly original, cerebral yet playful, self-referential yet open to conceptual interpretation—have always inspired reverence and the occasional shudder, even among well-schooled professionals. Since their appearance in published form in the years surrounding the composer's death in 1750, their audience has comprised principally those able to play or at least ponder their rarefied contents.

Both collections exemplify Bach's lifelong fascination with **counterpoint**, the ancient art of putting notes against notes, and his determination to explore fully the combinatorial and transformative capacities of his thematic material, oftentimes in ways that defied contemporary norms and tastes. A more specific biographical explanation may be offered as well: during the 1740s Bach had, for perhaps the only extended period in his professional life, the luxury

*Bach's* Art of Fugue *and* Musical Offering. Matthew Dirst, Oxford University Press.
© Oxford University Press 2024. DOI: 10.1093/oso/9780197536636.003.0001

of time on his hands. Early in this decade he relinquished (for the second and final time) directorship of the Leipzig Collegium Musicum, a concert organization he had directed since 1729. Repeated disputes with civic and clerical superiors also brought about a sharp reduction, from around 1740 onwards, in Bach's creative output as Director of Music for the city's primary churches. (This had little impact on weekly liturgies in Leipzig, since older works and music by other composers could always be adapted and performed at services.) More to the point, it seems clear that Bach had always intended to return to certain major works for either completion or further elaboration and to undertake new pet projects. Like a modern-day academic who goes on sabbatical to work on her latest book or a chef who closes his restaurant to experiment at home for an extended period, the longtime Cantor of the St Thomas School and recently named Saxon Court Composer exchanged some of his former routines to focus, during his "golden years," on compositions that afforded him free rein as a musical thinker.

At this point in his career, Bach was well prepared to think deeply about the fundamental nature of music and to capitalize on his own peculiar abilities. His long tenure in Leipzig, a university city famous for its annual book fairs, had provided abundant opportunities for learning and advancement, including the cultivation of relationships with academicians of various kinds, from orthodox theologians to progressive rationalists. Lacking a university education himself, Bach ensured that his sons had that opportunity; he also offered private instruction to an impressive roster of students from Leipzig University, many of whom—after earning degrees in law, theology, or philosophy—pursued musical careers. With musical knowledge that was second to none, Bach was one of the most sought-after teachers of his or any other era. An indefatigable industry and work ethic kept his mind sharp and his pen busy right to the end, it seems; witnesses recount his deathbed dictation of at least one piece (which will concern us presently) in the summer of 1750.

Of Bach's many musical modalities, **fugue** was among the most deeply ingrained. By the early 1720s he had composed twenty-four prelude and fugue pairs in all the major and minor keys and would do so again, for a second volume, in the early 1740s—constituting Books 1 and 2 of the *WTC*, respectively. For his final fugal corpus, Bach constructed from a sturdy yet pliable theme an astonishing sequence of fugues and **canons** that remain unparalleled in scope and sophistication. With its comprehensive survey of contrapuntal procedures and fugal subgenres, the *Art of Fugue* is arguably the most significant and novel undertaking of his final decade. His heirs certainly thought so: a 1751 announcement of its impending publication extolls this "perfect work," the likes of which "has so far nowhere appeared."

A similarly ambitious compendium, *Musical Offering* came about thanks to Frederick II of Prussia ("Frederick the Great"), who in 1747 invited Bach to appear at court in Potsdam. Imposing an intractable melody on his guest, Frederick marveled at Bach's ability to extemporize in the fugal style. Once returned home, Bach quickly expanded his improvisation into various groups of exacting pieces. The whole was much more than anyone (including Frederick) might have anticipated from such an unwieldy melody, one likely designed to challenge the venerable master at his own game. Unlike the *Art of Fugue*, Bach's *Musical Offering* abounds in contrasts, with terse canonic miracles juxtaposed in the original edition against an imposing trio sonata and a pair of keyboard fugues, one lean and rambling and the other a veritable colossus of counterpoint.

When they first appeared, these late compositional siblings stood at the apex of a revered but outdated practice, one whose luster had dimmed significantly amid changing tastes and the new musical priorities of a younger generation. As such, their joint mystique set in early, at least among aficionados of counterpoint and fugue. Hundreds of years later their contents still astonish, and their many secrets still fascinate. Few musical works have inspired comparable levels of inquiry into their original sources, proper

constitution, compositional models, stylistic allusions, and potential for meaning. The large literature devoted to the *Art of Fugue*
and *Musical Offering* thus comprises forensic studies of sources and
engraving methods, detailed theoretical analyses, and imaginative
interpretive accounts, but little for the general reader. This book
aims to fill that gap by leavening serious-minded musicology with
practical explanation and occasional forays outside the strictly musical sphere. Unlike many who have written about these celebrated
works, I have no grand theory to advance for either. Instead, I have
endeavored to provide—for readers both within and outside the
academy—an informative guide to the contents and significance
of both.

Bach's *Art of Fugue* and *Musical Offering* are perhaps best understood as his ultimate contributions to a lively and enduring
musical subculture, one that cherishes intellectual and tactile discovery in the act of composition and in realization. Both manifest,
in other words, a commitment to research and experimentation
at the composing desk and at the keyboard. Because this manner
of musical play assumes a certain amount of technical expertise,
Chapter 1 reviews the fundamental compositional operations
relevant to both works. This chapter also provides a brief context for the *Art of Fugue* and *Musical Offering* by situating them
within Bach's larger output. Chapter 2 surveys a considerable
body of scholarship to clarify what we know about their respective
origins and first editions, both of which Bach supervised. At the
risk of repeating information available elsewhere, I have fashioned
narratives and summary tables that incorporate the latest findings
while acknowledging lingering uncertainties that stem from the
muddled and incomplete state of the sources. The shared nature
of both collections, as comprehensive demonstrations of rigorously imitative (or, as scholars say, learnèd) counterpoint, further
connects them to a particular audience, as the latter portion of this
chapter relates.

Chapters 3, 4, and 5 take up individual movements for insight into related topics: Bach's systematic exploration of comparable yet distinct generative melodies, the habits and provocations of his musical tribe, and his manipulation of certain aspects of style, respectively. Both the *Art of Fugue* and *Musical Offering* are essentially variation-style collections, but their respective main themes encouraged dissimilar compositional strategies. For the former work, Bach invented a limpid melody that is endlessly adaptable and capable of numerous tricks, including artful combinations with itself and with multiple secondary themes. The latter's immutable "royal theme," on the other hand, obliges repetition while allowing for considerable adornment, principally via other musical ideas that surround and extend it. Chapter 3 narrates how Bach realized the potential of each in groups of related pieces that manifest ever more sophisticated kinds of counterpoint. A systematic plan for both collections can be seen most clearly in the first two groups of fugues from the *Art of Fugue* (Contrapuncti 1–7) and in the two ricercari and five *Canones diversi* of *Musical Offering*, all discussed in some detail here.

Musical gamers of Bach's day, the historical context for Chapter 4, valued canon especially for its artful concision and its mix of the cryptic and the facile. While this group's membership and modes of interaction have changed over time, the finest canons continue to inspire devotees; several from *Musical Offering* have also acquired extra-musical meaning over the years, thanks in part to the composer's well-documented fondness for esoterica. In comparison, the *Art of Fugue* canons play more competitive games, sometimes running on autopilot and at other times hiding their secrets in the manner of a musical tease, while its compound and mirror fugues pose formidable challenges of their own. Playing or listening to the lot requires a high tolerance for densely intertwined yet doggedly independent musical lines; there's even a bit of obligatory improvisation. Bach's lively sense of play, as expressed in both collections, engages dialectically through clues that are visible on the page but are sometimes hard to discern as such. By unpacking in this chapter several of my favorite "aha" moments, I seek not to short-circuit the game but rather to enhance the experience for fellow musical gamers.

Chapter 5 juxtaposes two comparable developments: Bach's idiosyncratic deployment of stylistic conventions and posterity's equally imaginative treatment of this music in tributes of various kinds. Bach had a habit of transforming discrete markers of style, forcing us to reconsider the associations typically conjured by such things. To illustrate this phenomenon, the first part of this chapter highlights two problematic movements: Contrapunctus 6 from the *Art of Fugue*, which sports abundant French-style dotted rhythms, and the Andante from the Sonata in *Musical Offering*, in which pervasive **galant** figuration threatens to upstage a delicate yet dense musical texture. The historical reception of both parent works, also surveyed in this chapter, is similarly a story of stylistic tinkering, though on a much larger scale. Here I chronicle a more profound shift: from re-workings of individual movements made in Bach's own time to the wholesale reimagining of his contrapuntal ethos in other media in the twentieth century. Such activity has expanded greatly the audience for both collections by offering new ways to appreciate Bach's achievement in them.

Chapter 6, finally, uses the unfinished fugue from the autograph materials for the *Art of Fugue* to meditate briefly on our desire for completeness or perfection in art. While the former compositional torso remains the subject of considerable debate, the latter ideal is ultimately of greater consequence, since our preference for "complete" musical works—in editions, the concert hall, and on recording—inevitably affects how we understand and assign value to both the *Art of Fugue* and *Musical Offering*. That bias, as I argue in closing, need not be determinative in our ongoing interaction with either work.

Although the musical examples included in this book will benefit primarily those who read music, non-specialist readers should be able to follow (at least in broad outline) the discussions of individual pieces from both collections. Translations of original documents are either adapted from those of the *New Bach Reader* (1998) or are of my own devising, and the standard *Bach-Werke-Verzeichnis* (BWV) classification numbers for individual works are referenced where it seemed wise to do so. Definitions for terms that are highlighted on first appearance may be found in a glossary at end of this volume.

Since *Musical Offering* (BWV 1079) and the *Art of Fugue* (BWV 1080) are best contemplated with scores at hand, readers may wish to consult reliable editions. The most authoritative full scores include those published by Eulenberg and edited by Peter Williams (both 1986) and those published by Bärenreiter, whose printing of the former work is edited by Christoph Wolff (1987) and the latter by Klaus Hofmann (1998), respectively, using texts from the *Neue Bach Ausgabe*. Two keyboard editions of the *Art of Fugue* (on two staves) may be recommended as well: those published by C. F. Peters (ed. Christoph Wolff, 1987) and Henle (ed. Davitt Moroney, 1989). Original sources, including the engraved editions, may be accessed through the Bach Digital online platform (bach-digital. de) maintained by the Bach Archiv Leipzig. An electronic edition of the *Art of Fugue* is also available on *téoria: Music Theory Web*, and multiple editions of both works are easily accessible through the International Music Score Library Project's website (imslp.org).

Those wanting to know more will find at the end of each chapter suggestions for further reading. These mostly English-language resources are largely academic writings that engage with topics addressed in individual chapters. Full citations for these and other sources may be found in this volume's bibliography, which assigns individual *sigla* (e.g., 2010a or 2010b) to multiple contributions from the same year by a single author, enabling the occasional parenthetical reference in the main text.

# 1

# Contrapuntal Pursuits

> In the musical ABCs, counterpoint is like spelling,
> as I learn to put letters together and, from these,
> form syllables.
>
> Friedrich Erhard Niedt, *Musical Guide: Part III* (1717)

Counterpoint, in a musical context, refers to the relationship that obtains between two or more independent voices, whether sung or played, in a shared texture. As practiced since the ninth century, when church musicians in Paris first added to a piece of plainchant a simultaneous countermelody, this way of making music remained at the forefront of the Western tradition through the lifetime of J. S. Bach, its most celebrated practitioner. Over the years, the wondrous discovery of those medieval clerics—that a melody could be made more beautiful when sounded against a secondary line—opened the door to multiple varieties of counterpoint, which manifest a wealth of discrete techniques and procedures and varying degrees of dependence between voices.

Broadly construed, counterpoint encompasses even the most rudimentary elements of composition. As Friedrich Erhard Niedt explained in 1717, it is principally a means to an end: one puts together individual notes ("letters") to make larger, syntactically useful musical units ("syllables"). His pragmatic and utterly rational description, meant to counter misconceptions among the ill-informed and the eccentricities of fanatics, takes as its basis the lowly triad, which is spelled (as Niedt notes in his next paragraph) by adding to a fundamental pitch two additional notes: the

*Bach's* Art of Fugue *and* Musical Offering. Matthew Dirst, Oxford University Press.
© Oxford University Press 2024. DOI: 10.1093/oso/9780197536636.003.0002

third and fifth degrees (or intervals) of its rising melodic scale. This produces *Harmonie*, as the Germans call it, a term that also refers to the way complementary musical lines work together, as harmonic counterpoint. Such things were the fundamental building blocks of eighteenth-century music, from harmonized chorales to multi-movement concertos, making genre an inexact predictor of compositional procedure. The essential point of Niedt's grammatical analogy lies instead in the necessary coherence of that juxtaposition of notes, gestures, or entire melodies.

A few other general terms should be clarified before proceeding to the specific procedures employed in the *Art of Fugue* and *Musical Offering*, whose contents and even movement titles reflect a highly specialized craft with its own vocabulary. In academic and popular discourse alike, both polyphony and counterpoint serve as descriptors for music with multiple independent voice parts, but only the latter also refers to the underlying musical processes that generate those parts. That emphasis on how notes are put together—or more precisely for the purposes of this study, on the various ways musicians of Bach's era invented and made use of musical material—prompts this initial chapter on the mechanisms and value systems of late Baroque counterpoint.

The pedagogical and practical habits of this era demarcate, moreover, a few general categories of multi-voiced composition. The **stile antico** or "church style," as enshrined by Johann Joseph Fux in his *Gradus ad Parnassum* (1725), stands at the conservative end of the spectrum opposite the more progressive, harmonically based counterpoint of operatic arias or concerted movements, in which a solo voice (the singer in an aria or the soloist in a concerto) dominates the texture. In between those stylistic poles, much of the Baroque chamber and keyboard repertoire is essentially equal-voiced composition, in which no single part in the texture takes precedence. Sometimes called the "fugal style," this mode of music-making obliged adherents to master rules regulating part-writing, as codified by Fux and other writers and as taught by practicing musicians to legions of students. From there the most adept progressed through short imitative pieces before taking on longer, more complex genres.

## Tools of the Trade

The fundamental operations of the fugal style include repetition, **transposition**, and **imitation**. In a 1753 treatise on fugue that likely reflects Bach's own teaching, Berlin music theorist and composer Friedrich Wilhelm Marpurg describes repetition and transposition succinctly, as exact recapitulation of a short passage and as reuse of the same material at a new pitch level, respectively. Imitation, the migration of a musical idea from one voice to another, often requires manipulating that same gesture or melody to fit changing circumstances. As defined by the Hamburg theorist Johann Mattheson in a comprehensive 1739 volume aimed at fellow composers, imitation produces a "pleasant competition . . . on certain formulas . . . or short phrases" whose intervallic structure may vary from one iteration to the next. Mattheson further notes that this compositional device assumes mechanical competency but "no great skill." Other writers on music from this time largely concurred: know how to concoct imitation, they told their readers, but do not pretend that it confers value on your composition.

This wariness towards imitative counterpoint reflects the era's continued fealty to a longstanding aesthetic ideal that shares the same name: since antiquity, "imitation" has also referred to art's capacity to recreate or refine the natural world. Theories of resemblance (or *mimesis*) therefore emphasize naturalness and clarity of expression as paramount goals for all kinds of art, including music. Because busy counterpoint could occlude music's message or meaning, critics and theorists of Bach's day generally frowned on the display of contrapuntal technique for its own sake: imitative devices, they decreed, should not trump the imitation of nature.

With German writers on music propounding this enlightened view, committed contrapuntists became easy targets: a year-long debate that Mattheson published in multiple issues of his journal *Critica Musica* ended with the humiliation of fellow theorist and composer Heinrich Bokemeyer in the face of the former's withering criticism. And yet, imitative counterpoint remained a routine part of compositional pedagogy, even in up-to-date treatises and tutors, since it provided an essential foundation for many kinds of music-making.

The Mattheson-Bokemeyer debate focused on the merits of canon, in which a melodic line is set against itself in strict imitation. This tightly regulated musical spirit, generally served neat, has long been a favorite of traditionally minded musicians, with distinct varietals created by and for individual palates. A less discriminating audience imbibes the simpler round, in which staggered entries of a short repetitive tune produce an infinitely repeating musical loop. Round melodies gravitate toward brief phrases of the same length and essential pitches of the home key or mode, producing a static but subtly shape-shifting chord as the various phrase segments entwine around each other: think "Frère Jacques" or "Row, Row, Row Your Boat." Canon generally eschews the singsong but is likewise premised on a single, inviolable theme in counterpoint with itself. Standing at the most restrictive end of the spectrum, this procedure mandates exact repetition of intervallic content throughout.

A melody works best in canon when it has been constructed with the intended imitation in mind, so that all resulting vertical combinations of notes are fully grammatical—that is, they produce no prohibited dissonances. Some canons also include secondary (non-canonic) musical ideas plus transposition or other transformations of the imitative melody. The latter may include **diminution** or **augmentation** (the halving or doubling of all note values in a theme, respectively) or melodic **inversion**, for which the Latin terms *rectus* and *inversus* identify right-side-up and upside-down versions of the same tune, respectively. Delivery of a given melody backwards, in **retrograde**, offers a comparable kind of artifice to the proficient contrapuntist.

Most one-off canons are notated in an enigmatic manner, with just a single line of music plus a sign, rubric, or brief instruction that identifies the entry point and opening pitch of the second (unnotated) voice. Additional operations may be similarly indicated. By preventing a quick read-through, enigmatic notation activates first the mind; the player discerns how a canon may be "solved" with the help of various clues (e.g., multiple clefs or key signatures) that provide guidance, if not a definitive roadmap, for successful realization. Unlike puzzles pieced together on our dining room tables, which tend to have but one solution, some canons can be resolved in multiple ways. Knowing this, adept practitioners value process and product equally, with the journey towards resolution offering potentially as much satisfaction as the result(s). Unsurprisingly, canon has always appealed to musical gamers, who once traded examples within their social circles, much as we might exchange prized recipes with friends and relatives. An enigmatic canon may also carry an inscription that alludes beyond the notes themselves, as several examples from *Musical Offering* demonstrate. By this means members of Bach's generation endowed otherwise insular pieces of strict counterpoint with meaning and extra-musical significance.

Fully realized canons, on the other hand, tend to be more substantial musical utterances designed to be read straight from the page. Working consistently in both notational formats over the course of his career, Bach incorporated canon into individual pieces and larger collections, some of which feature multiple canons in a single ambitious movement: one of the Canonic Variations on the Christmas hymn *Vom Himmel hoch da komm' ich her* (BWV 769/ 5) progresses through four distinct levels of exact imitation. By his last decade, Bach's abiding interest in canon had become an obsession. Even carefully engraved works like the "Goldberg" Variations, published with nine artful canons arranged in ascending order of intervallic distance, acquired more; his personal copy of the 1741 print includes an entirely new set of fourteen canons on the parent work's fundamental harmonic pattern or "ground bass." The two learned compendia that concern us here also include substantial helpings of canon, with four in the *Art of Fugue* and ten in *Musical Offering*.

Though likewise premised on imitation, fugue is not restricted by it. A fugue typically begins with a theme or "subject" in a single voice, which is joined gradually by other voices, each entering on its own with the same theme or a version thereof. Against these subsequent staggered entries, one typically finds either non-thematic ("free") material or secondary imitative ideas or both. To extend the beverage analogy, a fugue consists of one base spirit (imitation) with additional ingredients as desired: a contrapuntal mixed drink. Long before Bach came along, fugue was a broadly inclusive process; the term once referred to virtually any kind of note-by-note imitation, including canon. This makes a certain amount of sense, given the root Latin verb—*fugere* means to flee or to chase. A terminological distinction between exact and more casual procedures took hold gradually, which may explain why Bach included four canons in a work entitled the *Art of Fugue*. The modern understanding of fugue, as a genre that plays principally with imitative counterpoint, began to take shape in the early seventeenth century and became widespread decades later, in sources and discussions of keyboard and organ music especially.

Because a subject sets the agenda in fugue, much depends on the crafting of that sequence of notes. On this matter, in a 1708 handbook on musical composition, Bach's cousin and good friend Johann Gottfried Walther explains that one must "research diligently how and in what ways [a fugue theme] may be repeated, interwoven, doubled in regular or inverted form, arranged in an orderly, artful, and pleasant manner and thus lead to the end." Our standard vocabulary reinforces that melody's generative nature: the initial entry of the subject in the home key or mode leads to the next entry or "answer," which restates the theme on a related scale degree, usually the upper fifth or lower fourth. The original Latin terms likewise emphasize the functional distinction between those two basic forms of a fugue theme: *dux* (leader) and *comes* (companion or follower), respectively. The answer, against which the initial voice continues in complementary counterpoint, may reproduce the intervallic content of the subject exactly (a "real" answer) or may change it slightly (a "tonal" answer) to account for the irregular number of scale steps in the octave. (A subject with a leap of a fifth, for instance, is often followed by an answer with a leap of a fourth to prevent modulation to remote keys during the initial fugal exposition.) In a standard *fuga a 4* (for four voices), a subsequent subject/answer pair in the other two voices comes next.

Our hypothetical fugue may continue with restatements or elaborations of the theme on other scale degrees; modulations, interludes, or "episodes" that provide vital connective tissue; contrasts in voicing from one moment to the next; and any of the contrapuntal devices mentioned above in connection with canon. This array of options provides considerable flexibility and explains why fugue is generally longer on the page and more discursive than canon. Variety and contrast can be elusive, however, especially in a musical process premised on the imitation of a single theme. Bach himself acknowledged this problem by dismissing as "dry and wooden" the works of "an old and hardworking contrapuntist" who failed to vary his subject matter. As remembered by Marpurg in a 1760 issue of his *Critical Letters on the Art of Composition*, Bach also criticized as "pedantic" the fugues of another contemporary who "had not shown enough fire to reanimate the theme by interludes." The mere presence of imitative counterpoint, in other words, hardly guarantees a successful or memorable fugue, as Mattheson had warned.

Ironically, subsequent reception of the Bach keyboard fugues brought to performance of this music a comparable lack of imagination. By foregrounding all subject entries in these pieces, generations of prominent pianists favored the rigid skeleton over the supple flesh of Bach's keyboard fugues; their editions, which tend to include copious interpretive markings, reinforce the idea that subject entries are paramount in fugue. Despite more recent efforts to recover performance practices of Bach's own day, the former habit continues to inform our understanding of his imitative pieces especially, thanks to the dominance in music pedagogy of formal analysis, which privileges thematic material above other aspects of composition. We would do well to remember, as Bach himself insisted, that in fugue all lines matter.

One common combinatorial strategy in fugue involves a contrapuntal pendant to the subject itself, otherwise known as a "countersubject." This polyphonic *pas de deux* may move freely through any kind of multi-voiced texture, with partnered voices changing positions above or below each other and migrating to different pitch levels. Since the sixteenth century, the pairing of two rotating melodic ideas has been called double or **invertible counterpoint**. Triple counterpoint refers, in turn, to invertible combinations of three voices; quadruple or quintuple counterpoint extends the same process to four and five voices, respectively. In such groupings, attention must be paid to intervals between voices, since the inversion of a consonance may yield an unusable dissonance. To that end, treatises and tutors from Bach's day often featured simple numerical tables that translate intervals for the most common varieties of double counterpoint. From such sources one learns that in voice exchange at the octave, for example, a sixth becomes a third, a fifth becomes a fourth, and vice versa.

Triple counterpoint, a hallmark of many Bach fugues, is even more prevalent in the trio sonata repertoire and in other kinds of pieces with multiple invertible musical ideas, each with its own profile. Various rotations of the same three-part complex may furnish a structural architecture for an entire movement, with three combinatorial melodies yielding six possible permutations. Since some combinations will work better than others, composers learn to dispose these complexes judiciously. Marpurg advised intrepid fuguists to begin composition of a new piece by devising all musical ideas with an eye toward possible operations and combinations, so that the most profitable could then be arranged in a logical order. Composing in this manner requires, in other words, multiple skills: melodic cunning, mechanical expertise, and a keen sense of proportion.

Eighteenth-century music theorists also recognized distinct kinds of fugue, using a vocabulary that sorts and assigns relative value to the fugal subgenres by their respective combinatorial features. Both Mattheson and Marpurg describe a simple fugue as having a single theme whose reiterations are leavened by free counterpoint. A double fugue employs invertible counterpoint, which may occur consistently throughout (a subject paired with a countersubject) or arise latently, with each subject developed independently and later combined in a process also known as compound fugue. Either option may be extended with additional subjects for a triple or a quadruple fugue. A counter-fugue, a less frequently encountered subgenre, explores recto and inverted versions of its thematic material simultaneously. In the *Art of Fugue* Bach effectively merged this latter type with stretto fugue, in three densely imitative movements that begin with overlapped entries of multiple variants of the main theme. In so doing, he confirmed his bold agenda for the whole: in most stretto fugues, the close imitation occurs instead toward the end, in a kind of coda that supplies a contrapuntal "crescendo" just before the final cadence.

Bach's transformation of these and other fugal types in the *Art of Fugue* and in *Musical Offering* may explain why he bestowed on their respective fugues idiosyncratic titles, whose precise meanings in these contexts have long been debated. Sometime in the mid to late 1740s, during revisions to the *Art of Fugue* and preparation for its engraving, each of its fugues acquired the designation "contrapunctus," which since the fourteenth century had served for compositions illustrating one or another principle of counterpoint. As scholars have long noted, this was likely a strategic addition, perhaps even a didactic selling point for the original edition. When attached to more than a dozen fugues, it reframed these pieces for subscribers as exemplars of various contrapuntal manners. (The order of items in the edition, which is distinct from that of the autograph materials, clarifies the progression of fugal subgenres in the work and may have tipped the scales toward the less limiting term. Bach's manuscript copy of the work proceeds more by general categories of counterpoint, as Chapter 2 details.)

The original edition of *Musical Offering* includes two contrasting fugues both entitled **ricercar**, an antiquated term that carried multiple connotations in Bach's day. The earliest pieces with this title typically comprise simple chordal progressions with occasional flourishes; later examples, by contrast, are generally contrapuntal works in multiple sections, each of which explores a new subject. Though composers of Bach's day seldom used the word, the better keyboard players would have recognized these two general types of ricercar: Walther notes in his 1732 *Musical Lexicon* that such a piece may be an improvisatory prelude or a composition premised solely on imitative counterpoint. Bach paid homage to both possibilities, it seems, in his two distinctive ricercari.

## Tacit Aims, Shared Values

The extensive literature on *Musical Offering* and the *Art of Fugue* includes ample conjecture about what Bach hoped to achieve with these unprecedented contributions to a mode of music-making whose heyday had passed. A 1747 invitation to play for a music-loving king certainly provided impetus for the former work, although we have no idea whether the illustrious Prussian monarch ever opened the pages of his elaborate musical present. In a flowery dedication to the original edition, Bach presented it publicly to Frederick as a wide-ranging realization of the royal theme's potential, in compensation for the ostensible inadequacy (as Bach humbly notes) of his fugal improvisation at court. Years of independent research on Bach's part into the contrapuntal possibilities of a related though more congenial theme brought the *Art of Fugue* to fruition if not actual completion by the time of his death in 1750.

Bach chose to publish both collections by means of a painstaking process whereby staff lines then notes and all their usual appurtenances (beaming, slurs, text, etc.) are etched or punched backwards onto metal plates, which are then inked and pressed onto paper, yielding readable copies in the normal (left to right) direction. A popular method for creating editions of keyboard and chamber music in the early eighteenth century, copperplate engraving produces elegant calligraphic prints but at a steep price. Unsurprisingly, engraved musical editions from this time tend to reflect the best efforts of composers in the most popular genres. Bach's previous publications, which include the four engraved volumes of his *Clavier-Übung* or "Keyboard Practice" series, exemplify this trend with six luxurious keyboard suites or *partitas*, as he called them (Part I); an even more sumptuous suite paired with a model concerto for keyboard solo (Part II); a quintessentially Lutheran collection of chorale settings plus four *duetti*, all bookended by a magisterial prelude and fugue for organ (Part III); and a brilliant set of keyboard (the "Goldberg") variations (Part IV). Begun in 1726 with single partitas published independently and continuing with four composite volumes issued between 1731 and 1741, the series bolstered Bach's reputation as a virtuoso player and as a composer of great ingenuity and aspiration. Its publication made good sense, since this guaranteed dissemination among discerning musical consumers of some choice music for harpsichord and organ from an acknowledged master of both instruments.

In comparison, the *Art of Fugue* and *Musical Offering* offer fewer surface charms; they have more in common with Bach's unpublished keyboard and organ collections, the majority of which embrace a strongly didactic ethos through carefully curated models of a particular genre. Over the course of his long career as a teacher,

Bach committed to paper many such *exempla classica*: pieces meant to be played, studied, recopied, and emulated by pupils and admirers. The Inventions and the *Orgelbüchlein*—still familiar entry points for many young players—encapsulate his singular style in short but challenging pieces that encourage the development of good compositional habits while promoting *cantabile* playing of two-part counterpoint and facility with chorale elaboration, respectively. Such music provides excellent preparation for the more heterogeneous preludes and fugues of the *WTC* or more complex hymn settings for organ, whether by Bach or other composers.

The two learned corpora that concern us here seem more like ends in themselves, however, with play and study not necessarily leading to emulation. This subtle distinction may be inferred from Bach's teaching practice, as evidenced in original sources of the earlier works: the title page of Book 1 of the *WTC* (1722), for instance, commends its twenty-four preludes and fugues to "young musicians desirous of learning as well as for the pastime of those already skilled in this study." Had Bach lived a few months longer, he might have penned something similar for the *Art of Fugue* while directing its unusually demanding fugues and canons toward a narrower demographic of seasoned players. The contents of Bach's *Musical Offering* are equally formidable; its *Ricercar a 3*, the first item in the original print, is an openly subversive fugue, with extended chromatic digressions that fixate oddly on stylistic markers of the fashionable galant idiom of the 1740s. Even its sonata is comparably abstruse, with demanding part-writing and exceptional harmonic rigor throughout.

There is, in other words, some truth behind the familiar caveat that these collections are fundamentally "music for musicians." That said, in neither does the pursuit of perfection or completeness impede expression; both manifest Bach utterly in his element, serving up rigorously researched music that is by turns eloquent, dramatic, and playful. As his contemporaries noted, some with approval and others with complaint, Bach strove to improve upon nature itself by exploiting with every tool at his disposal the potential of well-crafted musical ideas. In an age that increasingly viewed music as needing principally to please, this pre-modern attitude toward composition had become increasingly outdated, with contrapuntal artifice shunted into music pedagogy and used sparingly in day-to-day practice. The old art nevertheless lived on in Bach, as the octogenarian organist Johann Adam Reincken famously quipped after listening to the young virtuoso improvise at the organ in the early 1720s. Little did Reincken (or anyone else at that time) know how this gifted inheritor of the contrapuntal tradition would eventually transform it.

Bach's peers recognized him as heir to a long line of industrious predecessors, from Italian Renaissance masters to leading lights of the flamboyant North German *stylus fantasticus* (the "fantastic style"), whose works accommodated layers of meaning informed by belief systems and intellectual pursuits that collectively lent cultural import and resonance to all kinds of music. "Soli Deo gloria," as Bach and his contemporaries inscribed regularly on musical manuscripts, echoes the message of the Protestant reformers: all music, since it comes ultimately from God, praises God. Even a clear-eyed rationalist like Mattheson embraced this mantra, noting in an early publication that the fundamental purpose of music is to prepare us for the heavenly choir. Alongside such religious messaging, Pythagorean and other ancient ideas about music retained their currency in the early eighteenth century: the organist and music theorist Andreas Werckmeister, whose writings Bach knew well, considered voice exchange in invertible counterpoint as the audible reflection of the whirling planets. Metaphor and analogy, as we shall see, remain eminently viable interpretive strategies for the *Art of Fugue* and *Musical Offering*.

At the same time, enlightened writers on music also harbored a healthy suspicion of counterpoint itself, with Niedt, Mattheson, and others decrying the jealous guarding of its secrets. And yet they encouraged contrapuntal learning, which enriches even the simplest music of this age. By no accident, music in mixed styles became the norm thanks to masters of precisely this kind of creative assimilation: Georg Philipp Telemann, George Frideric Handel, and Johann Sebastian Bach, just to name a few. The learned style, when pursued for its own sake, became either the domain of the gifted or a fool's errand, as the example of poor Bokemeyer shows. With few if any equals in this realm, Bach could occasionally afford to indulge his contrapuntal muse to his heart's content.

## SUGGESTIONS FOR FURTHER READING

English language translations of portions of Fux's *Gradus ad Parnassum* (1725) and Marpurg's *Abhandlung von der Fugue* (1753–54) may be found in Alfred Mann, *The Study of Fugue* (1958 and multiple subsequent editions). A new English version of the complete *Abhandlung*, as translated by Jane Hines and edited by Derek Remeš, is also available electronically at *Between Chopin and Tellefson: European Music Treatises*. Pamela Poulin (1989) has translated all three volumes of Niedt's *Musical Guide* (1710–17), and Ernst Harriss (1981) performed the same service for Mattheson's *Der volkommene Capellmeister* (1739). Detailed tutelage in counterpoint and its various manifestations in the eighteenth century may also be found in textbooks by Peter Schubert and Christopher Neidhöfer (2006), Thomas Benjamin (2003), H. Gilbert Trythall (1992), Robert Gauldin (1988, rev. 2013), Richard S. Parks (1984), and Kent Kennan (1959 and multiple subsequent editions), all of which include substantial helpings of Bach's music.

For a general book on fugue from the seventeenth through the mid twentieth centuries, see Roger Bullivant, *Fugue* (1981). Paul Mark Walker, *Theories of Fugue from the Age of Josquin to the Age of Bach* (2000) offers a comprehensive study of this venerable species of composition from the sixteenth century through Bach's era, while Laurence Dreyfus, "Matters of Kind" (Chapter 5 in his *Bach and the Patterns of Invention*, 1996) explicates its various manifestations in Bach's keyboard music. Multiple chapters of my own *Engaging Bach: The Keyboard Legacy from Marpurg to Mendelssohn* (2012), finally, explore the history of familiar performance habits in the Bach fugues.

# 2

# Origins and Audience

Sometime around 1740, Bach began to consolidate his compositional legacy through the refinement and enlargement of earlier works. Such activity gave final shape to masterworks of unprecedented scale: the Mass in B Minor, for instance, whose sumptuous Kyrie and Gloria (the 1733 *Missa*) he expanded to include settings of the Credo, Sanctus, and Agnus Dei texts (the remaining portions of the Latin Mass Ordinary). Though ill-suited to the Lutheran liturgy, Bach's "Great Catholic Mass"—as it became known in some quarters—provided an ideal platform for a comprehensive survey of musical styles and textures, from old-fashioned polyphony to modern soloistic writing.

Keyboard and organ collections were also high on the composer's agenda during his final decade, including revisions to older works and new projects. Following publication of the third and fourth parts of his *Clavier-Übung* series (in 1739 and 1741, respectively), Bach put finishing touches on Book 2 of the *WTC*, revised an earlier set of large chorale preludes for organ (the "Leipzig" or "Great Eighteen" Chorales, as they are commonly known), and published two new collections of chorale-based works: the Canonic Variations on *Vom Himmel hoch* and the so-called Schübler Chorales, the latter comprising organ transcriptions of movements from his own church cantatas. In addition, he found time for a high-minded if idiosyncratic royal homage and a systematic exploration of the fugal art. Both latter projects culminated in handsome engraved publications destined principally, like the Canonic Variations, for fellow connoisseurs of counterpoint.

Bach's *Musical Offering* and *Art of Fugue* reflect distinct compositional origins, however, with the former begun in improvisation

*Bach's* Art of Fugue *and* Musical Offering. Matthew Dirst, Oxford University Press.
© Oxford University Press 2024. DOI: 10.1093/oso/9780197536636.003.0003

and the latter most likely with pen and paper. Day-to-day compositional practice tends to mix these practices, of course, especially for those who play and compose fluently. Just as an experienced storyteller might later record and refine a successful yarn on paper, Bach reworked multiple pieces that began in improvisation, sometimes leaving a manuscript trail of different versions of the same work, each more fully realized than the last: multiple sources of the Chromatic Fantasy (BWV 903) make clear his penchant for perfection through elaboration and expansion. For his *Musical Offering* Bach quickly expanded an impromptu fugue into a diverse corpus of pieces dedicated to a musically inclined monarch, whose invitation to appear at court had triggered the work. Bach's familiarity with contemporaneous collections of fugues may be behind his *Art of Fugue*, but we know of no comparable initiating performance. Reflecting perhaps more than a decade of painstaking work, it seems to have been not quite complete at the composer's death.

Convoluted source histories plus lingering questions about the proper constitution and aims of both collections have generated, over the years, a significant body of scholarship. Borrowing widely from this literature, I summarize below what we know about the genesis and original environment of both works, leaving close readings of the music for later chapters.

## *Musical Offering*

Bach's audience at Potsdam with Frederick the Great looms large in the popular imagination as an archetypal juxtaposition of old and new, the definitive encounter between dour tradition and enlightened absolutism. Though potentially an awkward moment for the aging composer, the 1747 event enhanced the reputations of all involved, to judge from contemporaneous notices in the Berlin press. Its prominence in the biographical literature further suggests that its protagonists continued to talk about it for years. Bach had visited the area multiple times before: twice in 1718–19 for a newly-commissioned harpsichord for the Cöthen court (from the Berlin instrument builder Michael Mietke), and once or twice in the early 1740s, after Carl Philipp Emanuel Bach became first harpsichordist to the King. Bach *père* also knew at least one prominent official at Frederick's court: Russian ambassador Count Hermann Carl von Keyserlingk, whose cordial accommodation of the Bach family during a 1741 visit to Dresden inspired a tale about a certain set of keyboard variations, the count's insomnia, and a teenage harpsichordist named Goldberg. An invitation to Potsdam to play for the most powerful ruler in central Europe, who was also a highly skilled musician, likely proved irresistible.

Frederick, for his part, was quite keen to hear the eminent contrapuntist: according to reports, Bach had hardly stepped from the coach when summoned to the palace music room. He obliged straightaway, as one does for kings and queens, despite what must have been an exhausting trip of several days in a bumpy coach. A strong desire to please may be assumed. Bach sought royal favors and titles throughout his career, especially during his long tenure in Leipzig, where he clashed repeatedly with church and municipal authorities over various issues, from his use of assistants in church to the optimal size of the school's musical ensemble. A royal stipend or even a simple nod of approval from the Prussian monarch might have served Bach well as he contemplated the diminishment of his capacities in old age; his second son, who worked for Frederick and whose young family was growing, also stood to benefit. Sebastian Bach's long effort to obtain a position (even if honorific) from Friedrich Augustus II of Saxony had ultimately proved successful: he was named Composer to the Electoral Saxon and Royal Polish Court in 1736, three years after his gift to the Elector of the Kyrie and Gloria of what later became the Mass in B Minor. Was something similar on Bach's mind as he made the journey to Berlin eleven years later? A command performance at the Prussian court offered one additional (perhaps final) opportunity for social advancement and increased economic security.

He could not have chosen a more propitious environment for a late-career boost. Frederick, who styled himself Philosopher-King of the German Enlightenment, had ascended the throne in 1740 on the death of Friedrich Wilhelm I, who tried repeatedly to hinder his son's intellectual ambition and cultural pursuits—especially music, which he considered emasculating. Crown Prince Frederick nevertheless established by the late 1730s an ensemble of his own at Rheinsburg, in a palace suitably distant from his father's Berlin orbit. Once he became King, Frederick set about transforming the Prussian monarchy by adopting the manners and taste of Versailles, which since the days of Louis XIV had provided European rulers with a seductive template: absolutism with all the finer things in life, including a musical establishment second to none. Though in some respects just as autocratic as his brutal father (notably, in military campaigns), Frederick brought about a renaissance at the Prussian court by recruiting leading philosophers, artists, and musicians, including his longtime flute teacher Joachim Quantz, the Bohemian violinist Franz Benda, and court composer Carl Heinrich Graun.

Frederick presided over a court that attended on various royal residences, each equipped with a well-appointed music room where he could meet regularly with his court musicians. On the evening of May 7, 1747, the King had already picked up his flute for his quotidian musical *soirée* when informed of the elder Bach's arrival. Four days later a Berlin newspaper noted this detail in a chatty exclusive, perhaps the first report of an event in the just-finished royal apartments at *Sanssouci*. Its splendid music room, with walls graced by gilded mirrors and painted scenes from Ovid's *Metamorphoses*, was depicted memorably by Adolph Menzel in the early 1850s (Figure 2.1), in an iconic scene showing Frederick performing with Quantz, Benda, Graun, and C. P. E. Bach, all of whom were in fact present for Sebastian Bach's performance. With theatrical illumination crowned by a dazzling crystal chandelier and a clear division between courtiers on the left and musicians on the right, Menzel's painting depicts the illustrious Frederick very much in charge, with a select audience that includes his sisters Anna

**Figure 2.1**   Adolph Menzel, *Frederick the Great at Sanssouci* (courtesy of bpk Bildagentur, Nationalgalerie, Staatliche Museen, Berlin; Jörg P. Anders, Art Resource, NY)

Amalia and Wilhelmine, both of whom had considerable musical gifts of their own.

Invitations to royal residential quarters were rare, and the intimate size of Frederick's private music rooms—even this one, which seems larger somehow in Menzel's painting—limited the participants and audience for such gatherings to handpicked players, the occasional singer, and a few chosen courtiers. Evening chamber concerts, which did more than perhaps any other activity to promote Frederick's reputation as the quintessential gentleman king, generally featured his own and Quantz's flute sonatas and concertos and occasionally other chamber works. During these strictly regimented affairs, only Quantz, owing to his longtime service, was permitted to offer the King musical advice. One marvels at the sheer stamina of the core players: Benda claimed, with some pride, to have accompanied Frederick in more than 10,000 flute concertos. Such reports emphasize the unprecedented nature of the King's decision, on that fateful spring evening, to upend his usual routine and cede center stage to the "old Bach."

In an early biography of the composer, Johann Nikolaus Forkel (1802) gives a somewhat embroidered account of this epochal musical summit, based in part on information from both Wilhelm Friedemann and C. P. E. Bach. The former, who claimed to have accompanied his father to Potsdam, told Forkel that Frederick led his honored guest from room to room to sample new fortepianos from the Saxon instrument builder Gottfried Silbermann. With this detail, family legend took precedence over historical fact: recent organological research on the Frederician court (Oleskiewicz 2017) has established that none of Frederick's many residences had multiple pianos. Other details harmonize better with the palace's press release: Forkel reports that during their time together, the King set before Bach a musical subject that the latter transformed "to the astonishment of all present" into an admirable three-part fugue. Frederick's request for a six-part fugue apparently met with polite demurral and a promise from his guest to spend more time once home in Leipzig with the given theme, whose archaic nature attests the King's considerable musical learning. (Frederick's own sonatas demonstrate a more than competent compositional technique.) The court's progressive musical party continued the next day, according to the original news report, with Bach performing for the Prussian monarch and selected guests on the Wagner organ of Potsdam's Church of the Holy Spirit.

To judge from Frederick's own recollection of the event nearly thirty years later to Baron Gottfried van Swieten, then Austrian ambassador to Prussia, the King thoroughly enjoyed this opportunity to observe a formidable musical talent at work, perhaps in a veritable parade around Potsdam. Bach, who was well acquainted with the ways of royalty, surely appreciated the opportunity to play at length for a musically sophisticated ruler. Was there any more to it?

Some propose a political dimension as well, with Bach representing Saxony (which Prussia had just humbled in war) as a kind of musical ambassador, whose warm welcome at the Potsdam court was meant to send an implicit message to his fellow Saxons. While there may be some truth to this, one wonders what kind of conversation might have transpired between a middle-class cantor who spoke only German and a cultivated monarch whose first language was French; music was certainly easier to navigate and less embarrassingly fraught. Musically at least, Frederick had as much to gain as did Bach from this encounter and came to it well prepared, with an imposing fugue subject.

Interestingly, Frederick's retelling also includes new details that veer into the realm of myth. As reported by van Swieten in the 1770s, the King sang from memory his lengthy theme and avowed that Bach had "made of it a fugue in four parts, then in five parts, and finally in eight." Why would Frederick (or van Swieten) have embellished this story with such an implausible claim? Eighteenth-century fugues rarely went beyond four or five voices; even Bach composed only one with six. But an eight-part fugue, no matter how unlikely, enhanced the fame of an eminent musician who was becoming increasingly central to the nascent idea of Germanness in art. That connection, made explicit in Forkel's biography, fits neatly into van Swieten's larger program of Bach advocacy. The good Baron had been sent to Potsdam to negotiate the return of Silesia to Austria, and although Frederick refused to engage on that matter, the Prussian court offered other benefits to the cultivated Viennese connoisseur: the company of Bach's former student Johann Philipp Kirnberger and the latter's longtime patron, Princess Anna Amalia, from whose library van Swieten had copies made of numerous Bach keyboard works, including *Musical Offering* and a portion of the *WTC* that he later shared with Mozart. Van Swieten thereby became a primary conduit for Bach reception in a rival yet sister power. The putative improvised fugue in eight parts (a juicy detail retold at one of van Swieten's weekly musical salons in Vienna?)

nurtured patriotic pride in the shadowy "godfather" of the German musical tradition, while adding no less than Frederick the Great to his list of admirers.

The 1747 press account of the Potsdam visit notes further that Bach announced then and there his intention "to set down on paper" his fugue on the royal theme and "engrave it in copper." After just a couple of months, he delivered considerably more than expected. One wonders whether Bach began pondering the potential of Frederick's theme while on the journey back to Leipzig, perhaps while mentally reviewing his improvisation at court and planning its eventual notated form as the lead item of *Musical Offering*. In short order, he duly realized the King's outlandish request for a six-part fugue and added, for good measure, a generous helping of canons plus an expansive chamber sonata. Specifying for the latter the royal instrument plus violin and **continuo**, Bach may have meant for Frederick to play the most substantial part of the work himself. Table 2.1 lists all movements of the original print, not quite in their probable order of publication, for reasons that will become clear below.

For engraving of this *Musical Offering*, Bach relied on members of the Schübler family from Zella, who had produced other editions for him. In this case, the results of their efforts were sold in multiple printing units or *fascicles*, each with its own peculiarities, including individual numbering schemes and contents that may have been determined more by available space on the page rather than any intended order. The Breitkopf firm in Leipzig typeset the title page and preface, which functioned as a wrapper for the whole, and likely printed the rest from engraved plates supplied by the Schüblers. Exhaustive research into the printing process and intended order of items by Wolfgang Wiemer (1977), Christoph Wolff (1991e and 1991f), Michael Marissen (1994), and Gregory Butler (2002a) suggests a piecemeal project, with fascicles made available individually for purchase in any combination; extra copies of the title page supplied a cover for any or all sections of the work.

**Table 2.1** Contents of *Musical Offering* (1747) grouped by genre

| Movement Titles | Notational style |
| --- | --- |
| *Ricercar a 3* | keyboard score |
| *Ricercar a 6* | open score |
| *Canon perpetuus super Thema Regium* | puzzle notation |
| *Canones diversi super Thema Regium* | puzzle notation |
|    *Canon 1 a 2 [canzicrans]* | |
|    *Canon 2 a 2 Violini* | |
|    *Canon 3 a 2 per Motum contrarium* | |
|    *Canon 4 a 2 per Augmentationem, contrario Motu* | |
|    *Canon 5 a 2 [per Tonos]* | |
| *Fuga canonica in Epidiapente* | two of three parts realized |
| *Canon perpetuus [contrario Motu]* | fully realized |
| *Canon a 2* | puzzle notation |
| *Canon a 4* | puzzle notation |
| *Sonata sopr'il Soggetto Reale* | parts |
|    *Largo* | |
|    *Allegro* | |
|    *Andante* | |
|    *Allegro* | |

Unlike virtually all other engravings of keyboard or chamber music from this time, the physical dimensions of its various elements are not uniform, with the two ricercari in oblong format (the first in two-stave "keyboard score" and the second in full or "open" score), most of the canons in abbreviated enigmatic or "puzzle" notation, and the ensemble pieces in upright (folio) parts for each instrument. The result, as one recent writer laments, was surely a "bookbinder's nightmare." But this mix of page sizes and orientations (perhaps the result of a short turnaround time for the engravers?) was at least a practical way to publish music for the requisite performing forces, since oblong format minimizes page turns at the keyboard and chamber players normally read from folio parts.

Two months to the day after his improvisation in Potsdam, Bach assembled a presentation copy of three of the five total printing units and sent these to Frederick; the remaining two fascicles apparently arrived later. To this exemplar he added various inscriptions that make clear the debt owed its royal progenitor. On September 30 of the same year, the *Leipziger Zeitungen* announced that Bach's *Musical Offering* would be available for purchase during the city's annual Michaelmas Fair from the composer; other sales agents included W. F. Bach in Halle and C. P. E. Bach in Berlin. Priced at 1 thaler by Bach himself, who in 1730 estimated his annual income at 700 thaler, the original edition made available the rare fruits of a royal audience for those prepared to pay for it. Returning customers would not have been surprised at the price, having paid more for at least two of the four volumes of Bach's *Clavier-Übung* series. One wonders how many copies were sold, however: of the two hundred prints of *Musical Offering* that Bach ordered, he gave away the majority "*gratis* to friends," as a later letter explains.

In the edition's preface Bach admits that his improvised fugue before Frederick "did not fare as well as such an excellent theme demanded. I resolved therefore ... to work out this right royal theme more fully and then make it known to the world." Had he asked

permission first, Frederick might have refused: Quantz was forbidden to publish pieces he wrote for royal performance. Moreover,
Bach was surely aware that Frederick generally favored less complicated musical textures. And yet, the King had asked Bach explicitly
to invent a fugue, of all things, a request that may have determined
the eventual order of items in the original edition of *Musical
Offering*, which begins with a piece that captures the essence of
Bach's Potsdam improvisation and ends with the promised six-part
fugue. Titling both "ricercar," Bach acknowledged Frederick's desire for counterpoint while making clear to contemporaries the
distinct character of each: one loose-limbed and improvisatory,
the other learned and searching. In a last-minute adjustment to the
dedication copy, at the head of the fascicle comprising the *Ricercar
a 6* and the two final canons, Bach even added an acrostic that
affirms fulfillment of the promise he had made in Potsdam to return Frederick's favor with interest: *Regis Iussu Cantio Et Reliqua
Canonica Arte Resoluta* (By the King's Command, A Song [Fugue]
Supplemented by Canonic Art).

The two ricercari quickly found an audience, to judge from extra
copies of those fascicles printed separately in late 1748, presum-
ably for sale at the Leipzig New Year's Fair. Surviving exemplars
of the original edition, most of which lack one or more of its five
printing sections, suggest a savvy entrepreneur unwilling to waste
money reprinting the entirety if there was no need to do so. In the
most recent examination of the work's printing history, Butler
(2002a) proposes that Bach initially planned to publish just the two
ricercari plus a few canons, and that he anticipated more demand
for the former than for the eventual group of ten canons or the sonata, hence the atypical collation and asymmetrical distribution of
the whole.

Bach's flowery preface begs a few questions. Its linguistic tropes
became problematic in the late nineteenth century, as biographers
from Philipp Spitta onwards sought to rescue Bach from a ser-
vile position unbecoming a Great Composer. Some writers still

worry about its first sentence, which projects both self-abasement and a worshipful pose borrowed from religious practice: "To Your Majesty I hereby consecrate [*weyhe*] in deepest humility a Musical Offering [*Musicalisches Opfer*]." Though discomfiting for those who regard Bach as an unsullied genius answerable only to God, this conflation of temporal and spiritual sovereigns was in fact common in handwritten or printed dedications to eighteenth-century rulers, even when addressed to nonbelievers like Frederick.

More interesting than the verb is Bach's choice of the loaded noun *Opfer*—the word looms large on the title page in *Fraktur* (Figure 2.2), a decorative and vaguely Gothic typeface—and the explanation that follows in the dedication proper, where Bach avows that this "offering" grew from his resolve to compensate Frederick (whose request for a six-part fugue had gone unrealized in Potsdam) with a diverse corpus of music featuring the royal theme. With that melody now clothed in elaborate contrapuntal dress, *Musical Offering* "has no other purpose," Bach writes, "than . . . to exalt, if only in a small way, the glory of a Monarch whose greatness and power . . . everyone must admire and revere." And yet Bach

Figure 2.2   *Musical Offering* title page (original edition, 1747)

himself soon found another use for the work, as a gift for members of the Society of the Musical Sciences, an organization founded by Lorenz Christoph Mizler to encourage learned discourse about music—thereby demonstrating that even royal submissions can be re-gifted. Mizler's own gushing tribute to Frederick's musical abilities likely supplied Bach, in turn, with the very language quoted above, as David Yearsley (2002b) has pointed out.

Reading a bit more into this story, we might wonder whether Bach hoped for an appointment analogous to that granted him, if belatedly, by the Saxon elector more than a decade earlier. Alternatively, some have proposed that Bach sought with his *Musical Offering* to remind Frederick that even enlightened rulers must answer ultimately to God. All the "oddities contained in the work," as James Gaines declares in his popular history *Evening in the Palace of Reason* (2005)—from melancholy canons meant to glorify the King to a flamboyant church sonata laden with artifice— reflect Bach's worldview, in which religion and learned composition held pride of place. In such accounts Frederick plays the part of the imperious autocrat, "someone who plainly thinks of Bach as no more than Prussia's latest Royal Executor of Puzzles," as Gaines puts it. The assumption that Bach resented Frederick's outlandish request for a six-part fugue pushes other commentators further down this rabbit hole: Joel Sheveloff (2013) considers *Musical Offering* a "subversive manifesto."

Such explanations, while comfortingly egalitarian, assume that a lifelong seeker of royal favors and protection would risk not only his own reputation but that of his son (who was, after all, still in Frederick's employ) in an artful act of *lèse-majesté*. By effectively disconnecting Bach from the class structure of his day, these writers reinforce the familiar romanticized picture of a preternaturally brilliant, wholly devout, iconoclastic composer while ignoring his methodical engagement with the world around him, including absolutist rulers. At the very least, we may assume that *Musical Offering* was intended principally as an exchange among fellow practitioners, analogous to his subsequent distribution of the work among members of Mizler's Society. In tendering this exceptional corpus of music first and foremost to Frederick, Bach performed— one last time, as it turned out—a familiar ritual by means of which artists of all kinds made their way under the power of hereditary monarchs.

Frederick seems never to have acknowledged receipt of the carefully inscribed dedication copy, despite his enthusiastic recollection to van Swieten of Bach's visit. Given the quantity of tributes then offered to rulers from all manner of supplicants, from high-ranking diplomats to lowly farmers, and this king's comprehensive involvement in every aspect of government and statecraft, a reply would have been unusual, even for an unexpected cornucopia of musical loaves and fishes. One hopes that Frederick admired the engraved fascicles, if only in passing, perhaps recalling (while inspecting the *Ricercar a 3*) Bach's Potsdam improvisation or discovering in the sonata's second movement how the royal theme elbows its way into an uncommonly vigorous trio texture after some forty bars. Recognition in the form of either money or honorifics, as Bach knew well, was always iffy for services rendered, including musical compositions: he waited three years for the Elector of Saxony to grant him the honorary title of court composer, while the six "Concertos for Diverse Instruments" sent in 1721 to Christian Ludwig, Margrave of Brandenburg, got Bach nothing in return. Frederick's tight control of the royal purse frustrated many, from his own relatives to Voltaire, and one suspects that Emanuel Bach would have counseled his father not to expect anything in return. Bach's lavish gift likely found a more receptive royal audience with Anna Amalia, into whose library the dedication copy eventually passed. If indeed he felt slighted at all, perhaps the composer took consolation from the gradually diminishing importance of noble approval: Mattheson, speaking for his enlightened contemporaries, had argued repeatedly that musical value depended more on educated judgment than indulgence of the rich and powerful.

## The Art of Fugue

Bach may have begun work on this cycle in the late 1730s, possibly for his *Clavier-Übung* series, several volumes of which are comparable in ambition and scope, and perhaps in response to the work of other composers. Although printed collections of fugues arranged systematically were hardly common, Bach was well acquainted with at least two: Jean-Henri d'Anglebert's five organ fugues on a single (though rhythmically varied) subject from the *Pièces de clavecin* of 1689, from which he adapted a useful ornament table, and Mattheson's 1735/37 fugal compendium *Die wohlklingenede Fingersprache* (The Harmonious Finger-Language), which includes, among other things, twelve fugues that progress steadily through examples with one, two, and three subjects. The short and abundantly embellished d'Anglebert fugues may have suggested to Bach how a neutral theme could animate multiple fugues in different characters. Mattheson's facile and meandering efforts, on the other hand, likely inspired Bach's competitive spirit, as George Stauffer (1983) has proposed. Given the Hamburg theorist's earlier disparagement of learned counterpoint—notably, his argument with Bach's friend Heinrich Bokemeyer over the virtues of canon—and his 1739 request (in *Der volkommene Capellmeister*) that Bach publish a book of fugal models, the newly named Saxon court composer may have felt compelled, for a couple of reasons, to respond with a work that plumbs the depths of this distinctive mode of composition, as Butler (1983a) and others have suggested.

Autograph materials from the early 1740s include most of the first edition's individual movements, with several in early stages and the whole ordered differently. Detailed analyses of these manuscripts by Wolff (1991c) and others suggest an episodic compositional timeline, with work on the first nine fugues occurring sometime between the late 1730s and 1742 and others coming together over the next four years; Bach made final additions perhaps as late as 1749. Around 1745 the title *Die Kunst der Fuga* was added to the main part of the autograph by Johann Christoph Altnickol, who studied with Bach and served as his chief copyist between 1744 and 1747 before marrying his daughter Elisabeth Juliane Frederica in 1749. (The last word of the title was eventually changed to *Fuge* for the engraved edition.) Scholars have long assumed that the title came from Bach himself, who may have used it to affirm that counterpoint—and fugue in particular—is more than mere artifice. The composer was surely also responsible for "contrapunctus," an old-fashioned term that appears at the head of each fugue in the edition though not in the autograph materials. The semantic precision here should be noted: in no other titles or rubrics did Bach put such emphasis on the contrapuntal foundations of his art.

Table 2.2 lists the contents of the principal autograph and its various appendices. The former includes twelve fugues (corresponding to Nos. 1–3 and 5–13 in the original edition) plus the *Canon alla Ottava* and an early version of the *Canon per Augmentationem*, for which single-line and fully resolved versions are given. The two "mirror" fugues are both given in synoptic notation, with the *rectus* original unfolding at the top of each page and the *inversus* directly beneath it, so that the two appear as reversed images of each other on all pages of these pieces. Most of this portion of the autograph constitutes **fair copy** made from the composing score—that is, a cleaned-up version meant to guide the engraver. The primary composing score is lost, as are other (assumed) hand copies from revisions of individual pieces or groups; the portfolio assembled by Bach's heirs may have once contained additional pieces or fragments as well. Like the original edition, most of the autograph material assigns each line of music in the various contrapuncti to its own staff in open score. Exceptions are the two-keyboard arrangement of the second mirror fugue and the final unfinished fugue, both of which are notated in keyboard score (with the former doubled, for two players). Treated as appendices by Bach's posthumous editors, the latter items include a few corrections, and the final page of the unfinished fugue is sloppily ruled.

**Table 2.2** Contents of the autograph materials of the *Art of Fugue* (DSB, P200)

| Contrapuntal procedure/voicing | Movement title |
| --- | --- |
| Simple counterpoint | |
| *rectus* subject *a 4* | [*1. Fuga*] |
| *inversus subject a 4* | [*2. Fuga*] |
| *rectus* subject *a 4* | [*3. Fuga*] |
| Double (invertible) counterpoint | |
| at the octave *a 4* | [*4. Fuga*] |
| at the twelfth *a 4* | [*5. Fuga*] |
| at the tenth *a 4* | [*6. Fuga*] |
| at the octave in dim. *a 4* | [*7. Fuga*] |
| at the octave with aug. and dim. *a 4* | [*8. Fuga*] |
| at the octave *a 2* | [*9.*] *Canon in Hypodiapason* (enigmatic notation) |
| at the octave *a 2* | [*9.*] *Resolutio Canonis* (realized) |
| Triple counterpoint | |
| *a 3* | [*10. Fuga*] |
| *a 4* | [*11. Fuga*] |
| Mirrored counterpoint | |
| canon *a 2* with melodic inv. and aug. | [*12.*] *Canon in Hypodiateßeron al Roverscio et per Augmentationem* (realized and in enigmatic notation) |
| simple fugue *a 4* | [*13/1-2. Fuga*] (notated together) |
| double fugue *a 3* | [*14/1-2. Fuga*] (notated together) |
| Revisions/arrangements/additions | |
| canon *a 2* with augmentation | *Canon per Augmentationem in Contrario Motu* (rev. of 12) |

Table 2.2 Continued

| Contrapuntal procedure/voicing | Movement title |
|---|---|
| double counterpoint *a 3 + 1* | [*Fuga a 2 Clav*] (14/1 arranged for 2 keyboards) |
| double counterpoint *a 3 + 1* | [*Fuga a 2 Clav*] (14/2 arranged for 2 keyboards) |
| triple fugue *a 4* (incomplete) | [*15. Fuga a 3 Soggetti*] |

As was his habit for extended works, Bach spent several years revising, expanding, and rearranging the contents of the *Art of Fugue*. He supervised the work of the engravers himself, perhaps with an eye toward publication in two installments, as Butler (2008) suggests from evidence on the pages of the engraved print. But in the end, this sprawling project was not yet complete when Bach's eyesight and health failed in late 1749 or early 1750, and unfortunately, no one in his immediate orbit seems to have been privy to his overall plan for the published work. Sometime after his death, the decision was made to publish using the completed plates plus various manuscripts collated by C. P. E. Bach and his younger brother Johann Christoph Friedrich Bach, who was still living at the family home in Leipzig and had assisted his father with preparation of the work for the engraver. The eventual edition, edited jointly by Emanuel Bach and Johann Friedrich Agricola, was for its time a thoroughly eccentric compendium with obviously extraneous items plus an enormous unfinished fugue. As engraved by the Schüblers and published in 1751, the first print run of the *Art of Fugue* includes a short note from the editors acknowledging the incomplete state of its final fugue; they explain soberly that blindness and death prevented Bach from going beyond "the entrance of the third subject where he mentions himself by name" with the musical monogram B-A-C-H (German nomenclature for B♭-A-C-B♮).

When this volume failed to attract sufficient interest, its promoters tried a second time with support from an authority on fugue: the 1752 print run added a preface by F. W. Marpurg, who shared Bach's passion for counterpoint and fugue and knew him personally from a visit to Leipzig in the 1740s. (Marpurg may have encountered Bach again during the latter's several trips to Berlin during the same decade.) In his preface Marpurg commends the *Art of Fugue* first and foremost to those capable of discovering and savoring its "hidden beauties." Describing its singular nature, he notes further that Bach's "unusual, ingenious ideas" are "far removed from the commonplace, yet throughout natural" thanks to their "thoroughness, connection, and order"—qualities, Marpurg adds pointedly, that are rarely encountered in the music of other composers. The preface concludes with a noble aspiration: that these pieces "may awaken some emulation" in those who now write music mostly for others to play, and in the process "restore the honor of *Harmonie*."

The original edition of the *Art of Fugue*, whose contents are listed in Table 2.3, represents a substantial rethinking of the whole and its constituent parts. At some point after penning the extant fair copy, Bach added three additional pieces: Contrapunctus 4 and Canons at the Tenth and Twelfth. He also repositioned the third fugue in the autograph to serve as Contrapunctus 2 in the edition, and for this and the first fugue he added new endings, both of which extend their respective final cadences by just a few bars and allow one final subject entry to have the last word. The revision to what is now Contrapunctus 2 yields one other significant change: the autograph version of this fugue comes to a stop on a dominant pedal (m. 78 of the printed edition), whose central note A begins the next fugue (no. 4 in the autograph, no. 5 in the edition) with an inverted subject, making them effectively a fugal pair. This unique linkage between movements in the autograph disappears in the edition, where each movement (except the final fugue) is tonally closed. For Contrapunctus 10 Bach composed an entirely

**Table 2.3** Contents of the original edition of the *Art of Fugue* (1751/52)

| Fugal type/voicing | Movement title | MS No.[1] | BWV[2] |
|---|---|---|---|
| Simple fugues | | | |
| *rectus* subject *a 4* | *Contrapunctus 1* | 1 | 1080/1 |
| *rectus* subject *a 4* | *Contrapunctus 2* | 3 | 1080/2 |
| *inversus* subject *a 4* | *Contrapunctus 3* | 2 | 1080/3 |
| *inversus* subject *a 4* | *Contrapunctus 4* | | 1080/4 |
| Counter-fugues | | | |
| *rectus* and *inv. a 4* | *Contrapunctus 5* | 4 | 1080/5 |
| *rectus* and *inv. a 4* | *Contrapunctus 6 in Stylo francese* | 7 | 1080/6 |
| *rectus* and *inv. a 4* | *Contrapunctus 7 per Augment. et Diminut.* | 8 | 1080/7 |
| Double and triple fugues | | | |
| 3 subjects *a 3* | *Contrapunctus 8* | 10 | 1080/8 |
| 2 subjects *a 4* | *Contrapunctus 9 alla Duodecima* | 5 | 1080/9 |
| 2 subjects *a 4* | *Contrapunctus 10 alla Decima* | 6 (rev) | 1080/10 |
| 3 subjects *a 4* | *Contrapunctus 11* | 11 | 1080/11 |
| Mirror fugues | | | |
| *a 4* | *Contrapunctus inversus 12 [12/1]* | 13/2 | 1080/12.2 |
| *a 4* | *Contrapunctus inversus [sic] [12/2]* | 13/1 | 1080/12.1 |
| *a 3* | *Contrapunctus [inversus] [13/1]* | 14/2 | 1080/13.2 |
| *a 3* | *Contrapunctus inversus [sic] [13/2]* | 14/1 | 1080/13.1 |

(*continued*)

**Table 2.3** Continued

| Fugal type/voicing | Movement title | MS No.[1] | BWV[2] |
|---|---|---|---|
| Miscellany | | | |
| *a 4* | *Contrapunctus* | 6 | 1080/10a |
| Canons | | | |
| *a 2* | *Canon per Augmentationem in Contrario Motu* | 12 (rev) | 1080/14 |
| *a 2* | *Canon alla Ottava* | 9 | 1080/15 |
| *a 2* | *Canon alla Decima [in] Contrapunto alla Terza* | | 1080/16 |
| *a 2* | *Canon alla Duodecima in Contrapuncto alla Quinta* | | 1080/17 |
| Miscellany | | | |
| *a 4* | *Fuga a 2 Clav. [Cp. 13/2 arr.]* | 14/1 (arr.) | 1080/18.1 |
| *a 4* | *Alio modo Fuga a 2 Clav. [Cp. 13/1 arr.]* | 14/2 (arr.) | 1080/18.2 |
| *a 4* | *Fuga a 3 Soggetti [Cp. 14]* | 15 | 1080/19 |
| *a 4* | *Choral. Wenn wir in hoechsten Noethen.* | | 668a |

[1] Corresponding number in the autograph manuscript materials (see Table 2.2).

[2] *Bach-Werke-Verzeichnis* (Bach catalogue number) as assigned in Wolfgang Schmieder, *Thematisch-systematisches Verzeichnis der Werke Johann Sebastian Bachs* (Leipzig: Breitkopf & Härtel, 1950 and subsequent editions).

new opening section premised on a late-entering countersubject from the original fugue (no. 6 in the autograph). Its final location in the print may have something to do with its technique: invertible counterpoint at the tenth. Finally, a change in the appearance, though not the content, of several items effectively doubles their note values in the edition, mostly to avoid cluttering the page with busy sixteenth-note beaming; the larger values in Contrapuncti 8–11 and in the Augmentation Canon render each easier to read.

With these additions and alterations, Bach clarified his evolving plan for the *Art of Fugue*. To compare, the main portion of the autograph proceeds by ascending level of contrapuntal intensity: three simple fugues lead to a second group in double (invertible) counterpoint, then two fugues in triple counterpoint, and finally three examples of mirrored counterpoint, including a canon with melodic inversion and two mirror fugues. The 1751/52 edition offers instead reorganized and expanded sections devoted to the various fugal subgenres plus a larger group of similarly arrayed canons. With the addition of the appendix items from the autograph portfolio, the original edition comprises four (mostly) simple fugues, three counter-fugues, four compound fugues with multiple themes, two mirror fugues, the autograph version of Contrapunctus 10 (included by mistake on the part of the editors?), four canons, the two-keyboard arrangement of the second mirror fugue, the unfinished fugue (newly titled "Fuga a 3 Soggetti"), and the organ chorale *Wenn wir in höchsten Nöthen sein*. Although the printed canons begin with the *Canon per Augmentationem in Contrario Motu*, Butler (1983b) has deduced from barely visible revised page numbers that this piece was placed first by mistake; it belongs properly at the end of the group, so that the canons proceed by increasing complexity, as do the contrapuncti. Modern editors also tend to reposition the unfinished fugue before the four canons, making a contiguous series of fourteen fugues. This solution appeals to those who like their Bach with a side of esoterica: if indeed Bach considered the number 14 to denote his name, then Contrapunctus 14 makes an ideal title for the movement in which the family musical signature appears. (Following their numerical order in the alphabet, the letters BACH may be represented as 2 + 1 + 3 + 8, or 14.)

Both the autograph and the edition also manifest various symmetries and interior groupings. The former source's three simple fugues, which progress from a recto to an inverted then back to a recto subject, become in the engraved print a group of four with an internal subdivision: Contrapuncti 1 and 2 feature the recto theme, while Contrapuncti 3 and 4 employ inverted variants. The edition's order of the double and triple fugues makes a palindrome of their respective number of subjects, with three in the outer and two in the interior fugues, but the reordering from the autograph may simply reflect the desire for easier page turns in the print. The latter concern surely motivated one other change: the synoptic notation of the mirror fugues in the autograph (with recto and inverted versions reflecting each other on the same page) disappears in the edition, so that each iteration of these fugues appears on a single opening of two pages.

Bach's multi-year research into the combinatorial possibilities of his main theme apparently had no specific endpoint in mind, aside from eventual engraving and printing of the results. This may explain why one fugue lay unfinished at his death. He may also have sketched or planned additional fugues or canons of which we have no trace: a cryptic note on one of the autograph appendices, in Agricola's hand, alludes to "another basic plan" for the work. Does this refer to the distinct order of the autograph, or to a third organizational plan for the *Art of Fugue*, perhaps with alternative contents? The surviving documents shed no light on this matter; instead, they pose other questions that are equally impossible to answer. Why, for example, are the two-keyboard arrangements of Contrapunctus 13 part of the original edition? They add nothing to the collection's exhaustive survey of contrapuntal procedures and fugal types, and yet these pieces, which incorporate an additional free voice, are indubitably authentic and offer a practical demonstration of how other movements in the work may be adapted.

In the rush to publish the *Art of Fugue* after Sebastian Bach's death, Emanuel Bach and Agricola also included some obviously superfluous items: the autograph version of Contrapunctus 10 and the chorale prelude *Wen wir in höchsten Nöten sein* ("When in the

Hour of Deepest Need"). On the back of the 1751 title page, in what amounts to an apology for the unfinished state of the final fugue, Bach's posthumous editors explain that they "wished to compensate the friends of his muse by including the four-part church chorale . . . which the deceased man in his blindness dictated on the spur of the moment to the pen of a friend." One can hardly imagine a more appropriate swan song for a committed Lutheran church musician: with this final contrapuntal devotional, Bach made his peace with this world while preparing his soul for the next. But its inclusion in the *Art of Fugue* owes solely to his heirs, whose dismay over the incomplete state of Bach's final fugal cycle engendered a related species of musical consolation.

Hagiographic interpretation of the "deathbed chorale" set in early, as Wolff (1991d) documents, with one awestruck writer in 1754 finding it "miraculous" that Bach should have had the presence of mind to dictate such a work while struggling with blindness. Forkel's (1802) assumption that the alleged dictation occurred "a few days before [Bach's] death" added a poignant detail to an evolving story, while his affection for the "pious resignation and devotion" of this chorale setting imputed a strongly emotional tone to it and to the unfinished fugue, both of which Forkel explicitly connected with Bach's final hours. The story passed into the realm of saintly myth thanks to Spitta, who invented in his monumental 1873/80 biography a grieving audience for the crucial dictation. In a preface to the 1878 Bach Gesellschaft edition of the "Leipzig" Chorales, Wilhelm Rust gave rise to the familiar legend that Bach, in his bed and shrouded in melancholy, dictated a setting of the same chorale but with an alternative title, *Vor deinen Thron tret ich hiermit* ("Before Your Throne I Now Appear"), whose comforting text looks toward death and eternity as the humble sinner presents himself before God in heaven.

The truth is rather more prosaic: the austere prelude appended to the 1751/52 edition (BWV 668a) constitutes Bach's initial revision of a c1712 ornamented chorale from the *Orgelbüchlein* (BWV 641).

A third version of the same setting, which Bach failed to complete, appears at the end of his autograph of the "Leipzig" Chorales under the alternative title *Vor deinen Thron* (BWV 668). The "deathbed chorale" properly refers, then, to Bach's final revision of a youthful organ piece, one whose ultimate destination was not the *Art of Fugue* but rather another late collection. Tellingly, both BWV 668a and 668 expand the contrapuntal fabric of the original while radically simplifying its decorated cantus. Even as blindness and illness stayed his hand, Bach apparently requested minor adjustments as he listened to Altnickol (or someone else) play the final version of this learned chorale setting. Its associated texts surely provided solace to Bach and to anyone who may have been nearby, but the piece itself (in any of its versions) was never meant to be part of the *Art of Fugue*.

Though his earlier published volumes of keyboard music all begin with explanatory title pages, none has survived from Bach himself for the *Art of Fugue*. His posthumous editors therefore took it upon themselves to assert the value and worth of this collection in the edition itself and in various publication announcements. They did so in language that emphasized the work's comprehensiveness while reassuring contemporaries that it was "throughout practical," as Marpurg insisted in his 1752 preface. For this second print run, Bach's heirs also announced a reduction in price from five to four thalers, which seems to have had little effect on subscription numbers. Combined print runs produced fewer than 100 copies, only a few dozen of which had sold by September of 1756, when Emanuel Bach advertised the engraved copper plates for sale. His notice, printed in one of Marpurg's publications, reflects newly enacted restrictions on the use and ownership of precious metals at the beginning of the Seven Years War. Having concluded that there was no point in keeping such a weighty reminder of his father's legacy, C. P. E. Bach likely wanted another publisher to purchase the plates, but there were no takers. The cache of engraved plates thus disappeared, probably to be melted down, its metal repurposed.

As circulated in a few dozen printed exemplars and various hand copies, the *Art of Fugue* was known mostly by reputation during the second half of the century, when it served principally music theorists as an unrivaled compendium of learned counterpoint. Fugue found fuller exposition in Marpurg's *Abhandlung von der Fuge* (1753–54), the first pedagogical work to explore this mode of music-making apart from "other lessons of musical composition," as its author proudly notes. Emanuel Bach for one was impressed: his 1756 sale notice for the *Art of Fugue* plates declares that any intrepid student armed with his father's "most perfect [and] practical fugal work" and the "help of a good theoretical instruction book" like that of Herr Marpurg "must necessarily learn from it how to write a good fugue." Only then, Emanuel adds tartly, will "the secret of fugue" be liberated from "teachers who charge dearly for it."

## Music for a Few

In 1747, the year of his audience with Frederick the Great, J. S. Bach joined the Corresponding Society of the Musical Sciences, whose far-flung network of a few dozen members included such notable figures as Telemann, who was actively involved for several years, and Handel, who was an honorary member. Founded in 1738 by Lorenz Mizler, this society—the first German organization devoted to the academic study of music—aimed "to set the musical sciences . . . in perfect order," as its founding principles state, by synthesizing rationalist philosophy and what one might call "natural" theology, a blend of biblical revelation and contemporary aesthetic theory. Mizler, who also served as its secretary, was a socially ambitious polymath with expertise in theology, mathematics, medicine, music, philosophy, and law. Inspired by the Berlin philosopher Gottfried Wilhelm Leibniz, who used counterpoint as a metaphor for the harmonious motion of the universe, Mizler aimed at a rapprochement of the mathematical and metaphysical dimensions of music. He wanted, in short, to rethink the nature of music itself and align it with the current intellectual environment, which was dominated by the thinking and poetics of Christian Wolff and Johann Christoph Gottsched.

Eschewing a hierarchical structure for his organization, Mizler sought instead a conversation among equals by targeting each year a few influential fellow musicians. His success rate was decidedly mixed: C. H. Graun confessed in a 1747 letter to Telemann that "good manners" obliged him to accept membership when it was offered, though he had little interest in the society's agenda, while both Quantz and Leopold Mozart declined their respective invitations. In the end, Mizler had better luck with Lutheran capellmeisters and cantors.

A university student in Leipzig from 1731 to 1734, Mizler knew Bach well and was likely his pupil during some of that time. Acting as his spokesman against the criticism of Johann Adolph Scheibe in a pamphlet war that began in 1737 and endured until at least 1745, Mizler lent a literary voice to ideas that must have come from the composer himself. (Bach took offense at Scheibe's belittling description of him as a *Musikant*, a term then used mostly for musicians of low status like beer-fiddlers, and at Scheibe's criticism of his church music as "unnatural.") Mizler's society likely appealed to Bach precisely because of its embrace of music as sounding mathematics consisting fundamentally of consonances and dissonances. Having long steered clear of theoretical speculation—even while occasionally wandering the halls of academia as a distinguished guest—and after protracted battles with critics, municipal officials, and the rector of the St. Thomas School, Bach must have welcomed the opportunity for stimulating correspondence with sympathetic colleagues. His strong affinity for musical pedagogy, religious orthodoxy, abiding affection for learned counterpoint, and long friendship with Mizler made Bach an ideal candidate for membership; and yet, he joined this society only in its ninth year, when he became (deliberately?) its fourteenth member.

Advocates of a broader agenda for music found Mizler's Newtonian emphasis on intervals—how notes relate to one another mathematically in intricate combinations—a relic of an unenlightened age. Mattheson, for one, conceived of music more pragmatically, as premised on a network of "natural, moral, rhetorical, and mathematical relationships" in which nature held pride of place; mathematics simply helped her achieve certain ends. Mizler argued instead that the science of numbers could in fact open new vistas of expression for music. Bach's contribution to this debate, characteristically, took the form of notes, not words, on a page.

Paying members of Mizler's Society were required to submit annually a piece of creative work: a theoretical treatise or musical composition that could be discussed by members in correspondence and potentially published in Mizler's journal, the *Musikalische Bibliothek*. (This house organ, begun with promise in 1736 and inspired by the intellectual example of Frederick the Great, had a spotty publication record and only occasionally printed submitted work from members, leaving one to wonder how many members fulfilled the annual requirement. Its final issue, from 1754, carried the obituaries of four members, one of whom was J. S. Bach.) During his first year as a member, Bach presented to the society two works, one concise and the other expansive: the Canon triplex (BWV 1076) and the Canonic Variations on *Vom Himmel hoch da komm' ich her* (BWV 769). In 1748 he distributed among members copies of his newly minted *Musical Offering*. Declining health and vision likely kept Bach from making a subsequent annual gift of the *Art of Fugue*, as Hans Gunter Hoke (1975) first proposed.

Canon, a common thread in all these works, had long been a source of artful diversion for cultivated musicians, who traded examples in enigmatic notation with friends and visitors as musical mementos inscribed in one's personal *Stammbuch* or autograph album. Those with sufficient knowledge and experience kept a mental store of canons that they could reproduce on paper individually while seated at table with friends—as tokens of esteem, or as souvenirs on a journey. Canon functioned, in other words, as a musical game played by devotees of the art. Differentiating this insular culture from larger bourgeois practice, Yearsley (2002a) confirms that while music journals and instruction books kept canon in the public eye, its secrets remained the domain of initiates. Bach's "Hudemann" canon (BWV 1074) is a case in point: published in 1728 in Telemann's periodical *Die getreue Music-Meister* ("The Faithful Music-Master"), this odd-looking series of nine notes (Figure 2.3), swathed in an array of clefs and key signatures, elicited completion from various quarters. Mattheson's realization, printed ten years later, is just one possibility; Bach shared his own solution only with close friends.

In addition to the occasional canon for visitors and acquaintances, Bach devised multiple canons for various collections, including the two that concern us here. He also employed canon as a discrete compositional element in pieces that submerge strict imitation within layers of busy counterpoint. To cite but one of the latter, his *pedaliter* setting of *Vater unser im Himmelreich* (BWV 682) embeds canon at the octave on the eponymous chorale tune within a ritornello-based trio, whose upper parts meander chromatically (for what seems like an eternity) through thickets of **appoggiaturas**, long trills, repetitive *iambs*, and delicate triplets. There were plenty of contemporaries, including prominent taste-makers, who found such textures overly complex and downright confusing; they

**Figure 2.3** "Hudemann" canon (BWV 1074) as printed in G. P. Telemann, *Der getreue Music-Meister* (1728)

admired Bach's industry while questioning the practicality of his output. Ambivalence is clear in Mattheson's oft-quoted assessment of the *Art of Fugue*: this work, he opined, "will one day throw all French and Italian fugue makers into astonishment—to the extent that they can really penetrate and understand it, not to speak of playing it."

As it happened, a venerable Italian fugue maker already owned some comparable Bachian counterpoint. A package sent in February 1750 from Johann Baptiste Pauli, *Hofkapellmeister* in Fulda, to Giovanni Battista Martini in Bologna included a complete copy of *Musical Offering* and several movements from Bach's formidable sixth keyboard partita. In an accompanying letter, Pauli emphasized Bach's remarkable "dexterity of the hands" as exemplified in the enclosed compositions. Although we do not know what the esteemed Italian theorist made of this music, such transactions show that it continued to serve, in certain quarters, as music to be played, not just studied. For fans of the fugal style, the unusual difficulty of Bach's music became a central value, even a point of pride.

During the second half of the eighteenth century, hand copies of individual movements from the *Art of Fugue* and *Musical Offering* circulated among devotees from Eastern Europe to England, thanks in part to sales agents like the Breitkopf firm. Multiple extant hand copies of printing unit C from the latter collection (using Wolff's *sigla*) confirm strong interest in the sonata among circles of enthusiasts, who also rescored other movements from both collections. (Chapter 5 considers the latter activity within a broader context of reception.) Music from both collections occasionally turned up in published treatises and tutors as well. In addition to excerpts in Marpurg's *Abhandlung von der Fuge*, full movements appeared in several English publications from this time: Contrapunctus 7 in John Casper Heck's *Musical Library and Universal Magazine of Harmony* (c1780), canons from *Musical Offering* (with solutions) in A. F. C. Kollmann's *Essay on Musical*

*Harmony* (1796), and various items from the *Art of Fugue* in the latter's *Essay on Practical Musical Composition* (1799).

Abiding interest triggered at least two new editions of the *Art of Fugue* in the years surrounding the turn of the century, from François-Daniel Vogt in Paris (*c*1798) and Hans-Georg Nägeli in Zurich (1802). The latter even provided through notational means a kind of historical bridge for a generation of players who, like Pauli, considered such atypical music an invigorating challenge. For the growing number of pianists who were aficionados of old-style counterpoint, Nägeli rendered each contrapunctus in full score with a keyboard consolidation underneath.

## SUGGESTIONS FOR FURTHER READING·

Much has been written about the intended order and contents of *Musical Offering* and the *Art of Fugue*. See, for example, multiple essays by Christoph Wolff, as revised and collected in his *Bach: Essays on His Life and Music* (1991): "New Research on the Musical Offering," "The Compositional History of the Art of Fugue," "The Deathbed Chorale: Exposing a Myth," and "Design and Order in Bach's Original Editions." More recent perspectives on these fundamental matters may be found in David Schulenberg, *The Keyboard Music of J. S. Bach* (2006), which offers in-depth discussions of both works; Gregory Butler, "The Printing History of J. S. Bach's *Musical Offering*: New Interpretations" (2002); Michael Marissen, "More Source-Critical Research on Bach's *Musical Offering*" (1994); and in detailed prefaces to editions of both works by Peter Williams (1986).

In *New Mattheson Studies* (1983) Butler and George Stauffer address independently this prominent theorist's influence on Bach's late contrapuntal efforts. For a detailed guide to the scholarly literature on the latter repertoire, see Paul Walker's "Counterpoint, Canons and the Late Works" in *The Routledge Research Companion to Johann Sebastian Bach* (2017).

Among the many books on Frederick the Great, one stands out for its focus on his encounter with Bach: James Gaines's *Evening in the Palace of Reason* (2005). This highly readable work of popular history, with successive chapters alternating between composer and king, provides biographical and intellectual context for these respective embodiments of tradition and modernity. Essays by Mary Oleskiewicz (1999 and 2017), finally, offer valuable insight into Frederick's musical tastes and his collecting of keyboard instruments, both of which impact our understanding of Bach's *Musical Offering.*

# 3

# From One, Many

One of the simplest ways to make music from scratch is to repeat multiple times a single melody or harmonic progression, with each iteration distinguished somehow from the last. Renaissance instrumentalists were especially fond of this practice, which became during the Baroque era an essential organizing principle for multiple genres, from the humble keyboard *partite* to the grandly operatic *chaconne*. Bach committed to paper multiple variation-style works, from youthful chorale partitas to two late masterworks with deceptively modest titles: an Aria with Diverse Variations for harpsichord (a.k.a. the "Goldberg" Variations), published in 1741 as *Clavier-Übung IV*, and the Canonic Variations on *Vom Himmel hoch da komm ich her* for organ, which he had engraved in 1747 for members of Mizler's Society of the Musical Sciences. These two showpieces evoke the peerless virtuoso demonstrating his ability, whether for pupils and friends or in occasional recitals, to weave a familiar pattern or theme into a multi-movement work of astounding sophistication. By contrast, Bach's *Musical Offering* and *Art of Fugue* call to mind the introspective composer at his desk, consumed by the potential of more abstract thematic material. Bypassing the usual format of a series of formally related movements, he showed in each how a single melodic idea can animate a variegated musical corpus comprising pieces of different kinds.

As such, these late compositional siblings expand the boundaries of the variation set while still exhibiting unity in diversity, the guiding aesthetic principle of monothematic works. Adapted from thinking about art in general, this familiar ideal alludes in music

*Bach's* Art of Fugue *and* Musical Offering. Matthew Dirst, Oxford University Press.
© Oxford University Press 2024. DOI: 10.1093/oso/9780197536636.003.0004

to the potential of a well-crafted idea to generate, under capable hands, a single piece or multiple movements with formal coherence and sufficient variety. Counterpoint further requires a mind capable of thinking locally while engaging globally, so that the final contours of, say, a fugue subject emerge after thorough consideration of that same melody's possible polyphonic partners and its capacity for contrapuntal artifice. Pieces based on a hymn tune or a theme from a royal hand modify this process somewhat, mostly by limiting the palette of workable operations that might be visited upon or around that **cantus firmus** (a "fixed song"). But a pre-existing or imposed theme still obliges considerable thought before putting pen to paper in the creation of a new musical work.

J. S. Bach apparently had exceptional facility for this kind of thematic assessment, as his son Philipp Emanuel once related in an oft-quoted letter to Forkel:

> When he listened to a rich and many-voiced fugue, he could soon say, after the first entries of the subjects, what contrapuntal arts it would be possible to apply and which of them the composer by rights ought to apply. On such occasions when I was standing next to him . . . he would joyfully nudge me when his expectations were fulfilled.

With open-ended works like the *Art of Fugue* and *Musical Offering*, neither of which had a specific due date or obligatory overall shape, Bach had the additional luxury of time: perhaps ten or twelve years for the former and a couple of months for the latter. Decades of experience in this kind of painstaking work paid off handsomely, in diverse collections that demonstrate the composer's resolve, during his final years especially, to spin contrapuntal gold from almost any kind of subject matter.

While the respective melodic engines of the *Art of Fugue* and *Musical Offering* share a few common features, their differences required distinct compositional strategies. Bach's methodical engagement with them can be seen most clearly in the steady progression in both collections toward more sophisticated textures and procedures, particularly in the simple and counter-fugues in the former and in the two ricercari and central group of canons in the latter. This chapter therefore highlights those movements, leaving others for discussion in Chapters 4, 5, and 6. Various extramusical analogies, which add layers of potential meaning to individual movements and both wholes, will concern us as well from time to time.

## Maximizing Potential

As Bach himself explained on the title page of his Inventions and Sinfonias (1723), composition with multiple voice parts properly begins with the fashioning of either a plastic motive or a module of invertible counterpoint, which yields material for larger, more complex structures. His two- and three-part miniatures, he writes, offer "a clear way . . . not just to create good ideas but to develop them well." Armed with such music, even beginners learn that in the fugal style an initial idea sets the agenda for whatever follows, controlling the work's trajectory to a greater degree than does the leading melody of an aria or concerto movement, which may owe just as much (if not more) to a dynamic process or architectonic form. Almost any combination of notes and rhythms can be developed contrapuntally, as sources from Bach's era to our own attest: one current website tempts the budding if naïve fuguist to adopt its "simple 10-step guide to writing an amazing fugue." But a truly successful fugue subject requires considerable effort and expertise, as anyone who has labored to concoct one knows. In this regard, Bach's oft-cited summary of his working method, as reported to Forkel by one of his sons, is a useful reminder: "I was obliged to be industrious. Whoever is equally industrious will succeed equally well."

Although Bach himself crafted only one of them, the main themes of the *Art of Fugue* and *Musical Offering* have much in common. Both have two readily discernable parts, with a slow triadic opening followed by faster notes moving through various scale steps, some of which belong to the prevailing minor key's customary progression of half and whole steps (the diatonic steps) while others are non-diatonic or chromatic tones. Both themes begin and end on their respective tonic (or "home") pitches and are thus tonally closed. Their shared affect or emotional character tends toward the searching and serious; one senses in their similar opening gestures deep sentiment without the specificity of a verbal text. Such beginnings, ubiquitous in eighteenth-century music, revolve around a basic shape: a minor chord, typically a triad of three notes, delivered horizontally then flavored either with its leading tone (the sharp seventh degree of the scale, which wants to resolve upwards) or with its essential diminished seventh, often formed by a striking leap downwards from the sixth scale degree to the leading tone. Warren Kirkendale's (1979a) designation of this convention as a "pathotype" fugal formula nicely encapsulates its utility in works of solemn, even tragic mien: the Kyrie fugue from Mozart's *Requiem*, for example.

For the long-term project that became the *Art of Fugue*, Bach eschewed such drama in favor of a more balanced melody (Example 3.1) with two linked segments of the same length. Standing alone at the outset of Contrapunctus 1, this theme sets a calm yet purposeful mood: a slowly arpeggiated D-minor triad curves gently into its leading tone, inviting stepwise motion upwards and a brief descending melodic tail. The latter maneuver provides just enough

**Example 3.1**  Contrapunctus 1, mm. 1–6

rhythmic acceleration for an elegant handoff to the answering voice, after which two lower voices enter on their respective cues.

With admirable concision and simple contours, Bach's theme seems tailor-made for elaboration, transformation, and various combinations with itself. But we get none of that here. Following its straightforward exposition, this limpid fugue subject returns only occasionally in Contrapunctus 1, with well-marked entries in the most stable keys: tonic, subdominant, and dominant (corresponding to the home key's first, fourth, and fifth scale degrees, respectively). Strong cadences are avoided as the counterpoint glides through various key areas in graceful harmonic **sequences**. The composer offers glimpses of his theme's prodigious capacity in a few feigned overlapping entries or strettos (mm. 29–30, 48–49, and 55–56) but otherwise avoids artifice; even invertible counterpoint is lacking.

Secondary material instead propels Contrapunctus 1. What seems at first a casual gesture deployed against the initial answer (beats 2–4 of m. 6) quickly becomes pervasive, with chains of skips and suspended tones driving multiple episodes. Eventually these figures intensify the character of this otherwise serene fugue, whose final crest begins (at m. 63) with a prolongation of the dominant (a "pedal point"), typically a sign of impending conclusion. But a surprise lurks eight bars later, as Example 3.2 shows: a dissonant diminished seventh chord is left hanging, its partial resolution further isolated in sudden rests. Punctuating this pregnant pause is a tonic chord suspended above the fifth scale degree (in second

**Example 3.2** Contrapunctus 1, mm. 69–73

inversion), the classic invitation to a bit of summary improvisation. Performers may well wonder: is this in fact a written-out cadenza, one that began with the preceding dominant pedal? After an equal period of silence, another diminished seventh settles things by yielding finally to cadential pressure; as the drama dissipates, the tenor recalls the theme quietly in the subdominant above a tonic pedal. This little postlude, one of several refinements Bach made after penning his fair copy of the work, brings Contrapunctus 1 into alignment with other fugues in the collection that end similarly, with a final reminder of their respective subjects.

**Example 3.3** Contrapunctus 2, mm. 1–6

A new rhythmic detail enlivens the second fugue, whose beginning appears in Example 3.3. Consistent dotted rhythms and four-note slurs conjure a gently rustic atmosphere that contrasts nicely with the first fugue, whose smooth beginning recalls vocal or perhaps viol music of a previous generation. Players may also notice a more casual approach to the integrity of individual lines in Contrapunctus 2: after the initial exposition of all four parts, subject entries are not always announced clearly. In a few places, the first note of the theme is dovetailed neatly into the prevailing rhythms (mm. 45 and 79); it also appears here for the first time in F (the relative major) and in B♭ (mm. 45 and 53, respectively). A composite countersubject, meanwhile, skips casually from one voice to another, contributing to a richer harmonic vocabulary than in the previous fugue. As Benito Rivera (1978) first observed, this technique of countersubject "migration," which Bach used sparingly in other fugal works, permeates Contrapunctus 2 to an extraordinary degree. For listeners it passes almost unnoticed, since the countersubject, with its chains of dotted notes, is perceived instead as a persistent rhythmic pattern or **ostinato**. What Bach only hints at in this fugue he makes explicit in the next.

In addition to rhythmic alteration, the primary theme of the *Art of Fugue* invites melodic inversion, which permits changes to leaps or scaler motives to maintain harmonic stability: when inverted, a fifth may become a fourth, or vice versa. This standard maneuver nevertheless produces an ambiguous opening gambit for Contrapunctus 3 (Example 3.4a), whose first five notes vacillate between tonic and dominant minor harmonies. After lingering on the leading tone (m. 4) instead of the more stable third degree of the scale favored by the recto version of the subject, the inverted theme passes directly into a twisting countersubject with frequent syncopations. The latter idea, bits of which propel some highly chromatic episodes, imparts a restless character to much of this fugue; fleeting moments of diatonic calm occur only when it is modified or absent: the mellow-sounding subject entry in the relative major at m. 35, for example. Bach also manipulates this countersubject into larger shapes, such as the radiant soprano ascent to top B♭ in mm. 51–53.

**Example 3.4**  (a) Contrapunctus 3, mm. 1–6; (b) mm. 29–32 (alto and tenor)

Within this stealthy texture, the subject of Contrapunctus 3 acquires a suave new rhythmic profile, with melodious passing tones that match the countersubject gesture for gesture (Example 3.4b).

Interestingly, this variant—a local modification to soften some otherwise harsh voice leading—returns as the primary subject of all three counter-fugues. The presence of invertible counterpoint here also comes as something of a surprise: a simple fugue, according to both Mattheson and Marpurg, does not normally include such things. But Bach clearly imposed no such limits on his own work; his aversion to textbook definitions of the various fugal subgenres can be seen throughout *WTC 1*, whose fair copy dates from 1722. This lifelong "quest for harmonic insights," to borrow Laurence Dreyfus's useful turn of phrase, clearly continued undiminished into old age.

Example 3.5   Contrapunctus 4, mm. 1–6

Contrapunctus 4 begins with a different option: melodic inversion that preserves the original theme's initial interval of a fifth (Example 3.5). This prompts quicker modulation throughout, with mm. 2–4 already hinting at F major. Bach's disposition of subject entries in this fugue further suggests a pre-compositional tonal plan, in which he sketched out (perhaps in his head) initial statements on the standard scale steps followed by a second exposition whose four dovetailed entries follow an ascending **circle of fifths** (mm. 27–43). Subsequent changes to the intervallic profile of the subject (its fifth note in particular) produce some arresting tonal shifts: from D minor to B major across one barline. In the passage given in Example 3.6 and in two other places (mm. 79 and

Example 3.6   Contrapunctus 4, mm. 73–76

131), Bach harmonized the altered note with a dominant minor ninth chord—a shocking sonority in context. The episodes in Contrapunctus 4 are likewise unusually expansive, with multiple imitative ideas and subsections, all with internal cadences. As the longest of these (from m. 81) winds down, Bach slips in another kind of surprise: close imitation of the subject *per arsin et thesin* (on strong and weak beats), a technique rarely encountered in Baroque counterpoint, even *chez* Bach, who reserved it for the climax of his most rigorous stretto fugues, like the Fugue in D major from *WTC 2*. In the relevant passage in Contrapunctus 4 (Example 3.7), two pairs of nearly simultaneous subject entries require only steady syncopation in one of the parts.

**Example 3.7** Contrapunctus 4, mm. 107–110 (tenor and bass) and mm. 111–114 (soprano and alto)

The combination of a fugue subject with itself works best, as Bach knew well, with short themes that revolve around just a couple of chords: most commonly, tonic and either dominant or the essential diminished seventh. Though these are the precise contours of his *Art of Fugue* theme, Bach held his fire in the first several contrapuncti by merely alluding to stretto, as if to tease the observant player. The lone instance of close imitation in Contrapunctus 4—the last of four seemingly "simple" fugues—offers a taste of what's to come, with the following three counter-fugues accelerating dramatically

the progressive reveal of combinatorial possibilities. The latter feature (in order) a decorated main theme deployed against its own inversion in Contrapunctus 5, that trick plus diminution of the theme
in Contrapunctus 6, and finally both those devices plus augmentation in Contrapunctus 7.

**Example 3.8** (a) Contrapunctus 5, mm. 1–5; (b) mm. 33–37 (bass and
soprano)

Contrapunctus 5 begins with a novel bit of thematic overlap
(Example 3.8a): an inverted subject decorated with passing tones
(from Contrapunctus 3) accommodates, in its fourth bar, a recto
answer. Closer combinations open the next two counter-fugues,
both of which are similarly steeped in stretto. For Contrapunctus
5 Bach composed two back-to-back expositions, with the initial
alto-bass and soprano-tenor pairs of subject entries recurring (between mm. 17–30) in reversed order and with swapped melodic
directions. A brief episode leads directly into the first close stretto
(Example 3.8b), where different versions of the decorated theme
enter against themselves at the time interval of a half note. The
other two stretto options, at the time distance of a bar and a half
and at a single bar's distance, appear in turn (in mm. 57 and 77,
respectively), all in double counterpoint at the octave. Rigorously
imitative episodes in four parts lend additional heft and vigor while
focusing attention on an impressive display of stretto as this fugue

churns toward conclusion. At the end, a grandiose coda (from m. 86) gilds an already rich texture with a few additional voices that add simultaneous though cleverly submerged subject entries in the tonic major.

Bach's autograph manuscript continues with two fugues that became Contrapuncti 9 and 10 in the engraved print. Both continue the steady exploration of double counterpoint, the former at the twelfth and the latter at the tenth, but with multiple subjects. Double counterpoint at the octave, the pedagogical stepping-stone to more difficult intervals of inversion, occurs throughout the preceding fugue in the autograph (Contrapunctus 5), thanks to the relative ease with which consonant intervals invert at this distance. The increasingly restrictive nature of invertible counterpoint at the twelfth and tenth likely suggested to Bach his initial order for these three pieces. But at some point, he decided to group the double and triple fugues together and to precede them with two counter-fugues with abundant stretti, whose original order he preserved in the published work as Contrapuncti 6 and 7. The 1751/52 edition accentuates, in other words, his primary theme's versatility in various fugal subgenres and its capacity for contrapuntal artifice.

Contrapunctus 6, marked "in Stylo francese" in the original edition, speaks with a distinct accent, the result of omnipresent French-style dotted figures. Instead of a traditional fugal exposition, with each voice waiting its turn, this fugue begins with a stretto complex that juxtaposes three overlapped iterations of its subject (Example 3.9): in order of appearance, an initial recto subject then two in diminution, one inverted and the other recto. (The atypical beginning, as David Schulenberg observes, may explain

**Example 3.9** Contrapunctus 6, mm. 1–5

Bach's eventual title of "contrapunctus" for all the fugues.) A extravagantly imitative counter-fugue follows. Invertible combinations and diminutions thereof permeate the texture so thoroughly that some episodes are barely perceptible as such, prompting Donald Francis Tovey's apt description of it as "a solid mass of stretto."

With busy independent parts crowded together at some moments and separated widely at others, this is the thorniest item thus far in the collection, a formidable challenge for even a highly skilled pair of hands. Streams of flowing sixteenth notes eventually offer relief from the relentless dotted notes and quick upbeats, the familiar markers of French Baroque style, but do little to lessen the overall intensity. The most *ouverture*-like passage comes late in the game, with the dotted figures asserting full control (from m. 71) just before a dramatic hold or "fermata." Out of the latter's elongated dominant seventh springs a proudly rhetorical flourish that lands on a tonic pedal, above which is yet one more combination of multiple subject entries at various rhythmic levels, with additional voices enriching the texture at the very end. No French composer could have dreamt this up.

Contrapunctus 7 begins with a similar combination of three overlapped subject entries with two in diminution, underneath which emerges an augmentation of the now-pervasive dotted variant of the main theme. This glacial cantus firmus, whose first appearance in the bass (at m. 5) commands attention, rises gradually through the stretto-drenched texture in four alternating inverted and recto iterations. Its final clarion statement in the soprano introduces a brief but expertly calibrated bit of keyboard recitative (mm. 58–59), which leavens the ritual procession with a bit of spontaneity (as A. E. F. Dickinson once remarked). So dense is the constant barrage of diminutions that the three rhythmically unaltered subject entries are virtually inaudible. Incredibly, there is but a single short episode.

To summarize: in the first seven contrapuncti of the *Art of Fugue*, Bach puts an unpretentious yet fecund theme through its paces in four simple fugues and three counter-fugues, each more technically advanced and digitally challenging than the last. Manipulations of the primary theme include small rhythmic adjustments, complementary ideas, contrary motion or melodic inversion, and a full range of additional devices including stretto, diminution, and augmentation. The steady increase in complexity encourages a mode of engagement attuned to this collection's peculiar fusion of pedagogical instruction with music of the highest art, as Spitta first pointed out. Fugues from the *WTC*, to compare, have no intrinsic connection to each other; quite a few evince comparable ambition, but there is no discernable logic to the order of fugues in either Book 1 or Book 2. Bach's *Art of Fugue*, unusually, comprises a systematic cycle of pieces generated from a single theme with seemingly endless capacity for adaptation and combination.

## Being Subject to a Theme

The "fashionably sinuous" royal theme of *Musical Offering* (Figure 3.1), to borrow Peter Williams's pithy description, begins with a triadic gesture comparable to that of the *Art of Fugue* theme, to which Frederick added a dissonant detour: a bolt downwards from the sixth scale degree to the leading tone. The resulting diminished seventh—a *saltus duriusculus* or "difficult leap," as the seventeenth-century German theorist Christoph Bernhard christened this interval in a seminal treatise on musical rhetoric—serves in texted

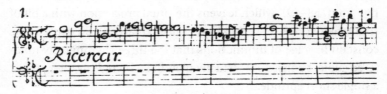

**Figure 3.1** *Ricercar a 3* from *Musical Offering*, mm. 1–11 (original edition, 1747)

works from this time to amplify sorrowful or sometimes frightful concepts: "And with His Stripes" from Handel's *Messiah*, for instance, which recalls the ghastly wounds of Jesus's scourging. The royal theme's second half puts this melody in a league of its own, however. Like many a royal pronouncement, Frederick's high-flown melody relies on lofty rhetoric, with a dramatic pause cleaving it in two and delaying purposefully the inevitable. Tonal closure comes only after a lengthy chromatic descent from the fifth scale degree to the tonic note.

This theme's big personality has caused many to wonder whether Frederick intended it to stump his distinguished guest. Bach surely relied during his Potsdam improvisation on a lifetime of experience with similar melodies, including those that drive several fugues from the *WTC* (Book 1: G minor; Book 2: F minor and A minor) and at least one organ fugue (BWV 537/2). Three of four canons in the *Art of Fugue* embrace the defining diminished seventh as well, either directly or across the distance of a couple of bars. One wonders whether Bach recalled, while contemplating the royal theme, his cousin Johann Gottfried Walther's association of such patterns with "lowly, insignificant, and disdainful things." The 1747 newspaper report claims instead that Bach found it "exceedingly beautiful," language he never used for any other melody, as Christoph Wolff (1991a) has pointed out. Other music historians have proposed that the King sought input in advance from his court musicians, so that he might temper his musical taste toward something more appropriate for a master of the fugal style. But with only Quantz allowed to dispense advice on Frederick's compositions, that seems unlikely, especially for a famous visitor whose Potsdam appearance attracted the attention of the local press. And yet, similarities between the royal theme and various contrapuntal ideas of Quantz and others continue to sustain this line of inquiry.

Its authorship aside, this grandiose melody wears its learning proudly, as befits both an enlightened philosopher-king and an expert contrapuntist. An initial series of even half-notes or "breves," in the reserved style of the stile antico, leads (after the surprise of the diminished seventh and the ensuing rest) to a winding but goal-oriented subject tail whose longest note ushers in a decisive closing gesture: a double cadence to the tonic pitch, reinforced by an ornament on the penultimate note. Marpurg, for one, would not have approved; his *Abhandlung von der Fuge* advises against ending a subject with a perfect cadence. Bach, however, was obliged to continue straightaway, and he did so with aplomb.

At this point in the *Ricercar a 3*, as its initial subject entry concludes, a sudden shift in style occurs. Quick movement to the dominant becomes necessary for the fugal answer, which needs to enter a fourth below (not a fifth above) because of the high tessitura. Bach's solution avoids a forbidden open fourth on the downbeat of the ninth bar but creates a contrapuntal "hiccough," as one wag calls it, as the subject's last note dovetails into a tapped-out series of modulating staccato quarter notes that have little to do with the royal theme. To compare, the *Ricercar a 6* begins more sensibly on "middle" C, from which the answer proceeds directly at the raised fifth without an intervening bar. For the improvisation that begat the *Ricercar a 3*, did Frederick simply lean over or around Bach to play his royal theme on the treble end of the instrument? A considerate guest would continue directly, without shifting registers.

Though the staccato notes in mm. 9–11 may not have provided workable material for a consistent countersubject (as mm. 23–24 demonstrate), Bach swiftly incorporated elsewhere this motive redolent of the galant, a mid-century style that relied on repetitive gestures to accompany tuneful melodies (see the first episode, from m. 18). At subsequent entries of the royal theme, motives are mixed freely, with figuration that wanders through various rhythmic patterns, as improvisations tend to do. The *Ricercar a 3* has additional voicing idiosyncrasies throughout, with upper and middle voices often riding well above a bass line that rumbles occasionally toward the bottom of the keyboard, giving the right hand more than its fair share of the three-part texture. Other Bach fugues *a 3* avoid such widely spaced voicing either with motivically conceived subjects of smaller overall ambitus or range (e.g., *WTC 1* Fugues in C minor or E major) or with long stretches of just two active voices (Fugues in C♯ major or G major from the same volume). Closest to the *Ricercar a 3* in overall style is the Fugue in E minor from *WTC 2*, whose rambling subject, mix of duple and triple subdivisions, and consistently full voicing make for a comparable challenge, even for experienced players. But unlike these fugues of Bach's own invention, whose subjects he could tinker with and refine, a royally conferred theme obliges compliance. Even if he made small modifications to it, Bach was saddled with a regal yet ruminative melody comprising a solemn preamble, a serpentine midsection, and a forthright conclusion.

Any contrapuntal adornment, as he must have realized straightaway, would have to revolve around this cantus firmus, not depend on its capacity for learned devices. Unsurprisingly, the two ricercari in *Musical Offering* comprise much beautifully crafted counterpoint but no fancy tricks like stretto or melodic inversion. That said, the opening gesture of the royal theme adapts well to harmonic sequence. Bach took advantage right away in the *Ricercar a 3*, on the heels of its initial exposition, with two "false" entries in the bass (mm. 38 and 40) accompanied by sudden triplet figuration above. These brief thematic peals lead to a short sequential passage with outer voices moving in contrary motion (mm. 42–45), after which the complete subject returns for successive entries in G minor (m. 46), C minor (m. 59), and F minor (m. 72), each likewise followed with modulatory figuration. Some of this material is then repeated in transposition, a skill beloved by improvisers especially. (Compare mm. 38–53 with 87–102, allowing for some invertible swapping in the upper parts.) Bach made one other modification, in a couple of places, to the royal theme: a small but conspicuous displacement of its final pitch, the second of which (at m. 103) brings this fugue to a secondary dominant pedal that cadences, after some further noodling, in G minor (m. 109).

From this point onwards, the *Ricercar a 3* becomes a veritable push-me-pull-you of imitative motives laden with appoggiaturas ("sigh" figures) and chromatic motives, which together dominate the texture until the complete subject finally emerges from the modulatory miasma in the soprano voice and in the tonic key, to boot (m. 141). Two more statements of the theme, one in the dominant (alto) and the other in the tonic (bass), precede a dominant pedal (from m. 180) that recapitulates in transposition the midpoint cadential preparation. Here, however, the pedal point leads to an extended final cadence with a drawn-out double appoggiatura in the right hand.

Strategically, the curious ending makes sense, since it obliges the player to continue into the collection, leaving behind the "rather strange digressions" of the *Ricercar a 3*, which writers since Spitta have excused as somehow unworthy or at least uncharacteristic of Bach, evidence of "the influence of . . . external circumstances." (Hans T. David continued this line of criticism in his 1945 book on *Musical Offering* by regretting the "lack of balance" in the work.) But Bach's quirky sense of humor may be interpreted more generously: his *Ricercar a 3* is effectively a cunning pastiche, in which a grandly learned theme from the consummate *galant homme* mingles provocatively with stylish decoration from the great master of fugue. Awarded pride of place in the original edition, it demonstrates Bach's ability to assimilate disparate styles within a strongly contrapuntal framework. Alongside his trademark ingenuity with the notes themselves, this discursive fugue accentuates Bach's considerable musical *Witz*—the characteristically German affection for wit or humor achieved through superior knowledge and application—and his willingness to work with an imposed theme.

The *Ricercar a 6* fares better in the literature thanks to a more consistent musical ethos, which sits within the critical comfort zone of stile antico polyphony. An unusually luxurious piece of counterpoint, this fugue shares its fulsome texture with just one other work by Bach for a single player: an organ setting of the chorale *Aus tiefer Not schrei' ich zu dir* (BWV 686) with six parts divided between the hands and feet. As in that famously dense organ chorale, initial exposition of the royal theme in the *Ricercar a 6* is by-the-book, with no filler between the first four statements of the theme; the remaining two entries require just a couple of additional bars each for sequential movement to the necessary pitches. Six more subject entries occur in this lengthy fugue (one in each voice), and as in the *Ricercar a 3*, Bach lets the royal theme speak for itself, without alteration or close combination with itself.

Though its conventional exposition and its subsequent restatements of the royal theme on various scale degrees signal fugue, the *Ricercar a 6* also incorporates key features of its namesake, the contrapuntal ricercar: namely, periodic strong cadences and new points of imitation that define multiple sections within the work. The latter function as fugal episodes, with motives that come and go, some falling into canonic or simultaneous imitation and others combining to produce mini-permutation fugues, in which multiple melodic cells strung together horizontally are closely overlapped with the same series of notes in the other parts. Echoes of the royal theme's head motive and chromatic tail are pervasive, as are allusions to other works of Bach: the first episode of the *Ricercar a 6* (from m. 29 of the printed version) recalls the "Gravement" section of the *Pièce d'orgue* (BWV 572), while the motivic material of its last episode (from m. 90 of the printed version) resembles the subject of the Fugue in A♭ major from *WTC 2*. For those who notice the references, a valedictory reading is hard to resist.

Allegorical interpretations of the *Ricercar a 6*, on the other hand, draw on religion and classical literature for insight into its singular nature and affective argument. Zoltán Göncz (2011), for example, considers this piece an elaborate musical meditation on the Ten Commandments. When reading such a detailed exegesis, a willingness to believe becomes essential, since most of the melodic figures that Göncz cites as representing this or that commandment are in fact conventional combinations of notes. Many of the parallel passages he summons from other works of Bach (both texted and untexted) seem, moreover, to convey other messages. Most imaginatively, Göncz asserts that the motive of the first episode in the *Ricercar a 6* (from m. 29 of the original edition) "keeps the Sabbath" by piously avoiding the otherwise essential work done by all other secondary figures in this work: accompanying the royal theme.

Michael Marissen's similarly theological yet more nuanced reading of the entire work (1995) proposes that *Musical Offering* is infused throughout with melancholy affect. This collection, Marissen argues, reflects a quintessentially Lutheran worldview of "glorification in abasement" and thus constitutes a spiritually infused musical rejoinder to Frederick. Relying on an equally venerable source, Warren Kirkendale (1979b and 1997) and Ursula Kirkendale (1980) describe both ricercari as exhortatory preludes to different sections of *Musical Offering*, which, they propose, follows an order inspired by Quintilian's *Institutio oratoria*. The *Ricercar a 6*, in their elaborate rhetorical scheme, constitutes the work's second *exordium* or *insinuatio*, in which the argument of an oration (as described by Cicero) emerges through inference and insinuation rather than direct appeal. Among other features of the work, the Kirkendales point to subject entries in this piece that Bach embedded discretely within a sonorous matrix of imitative counterpoint.

Ruth HaCohen (2006) has called attention to the central problem with such interpretive strategies, which are legion for *Musical Offering* thanks to its eccentric mix of styles and genres and lingering questions about the intended order of items in the original edition. Probing our reliance on allegorical readings of this work in particular, HaCohen maintains that it was created in and continues to occupy a liminal space, one that resists totalizing explanations. More generally, she reminds us that even the most meticulously constructed and historically relevant analogy, though potentially useful as a hermeneutic tool to stimulate the imagination and foster new ways of understanding, has a limited shelf life. That said, broadly contextual readings can enrich a reader's understanding of problematic or iconic works, even if our larger musical culture prefers artistic layering—organ recitals with light shows or staged presentations of the Bach passions—to determinative interpretations. The assumption that we may access intentions by mapping a belief system or mode of thought onto an individual utterance or action has been with us for most of human history, despite attempts to dismantle this or that hypothesis. Insular musical works like *Musical Offering* will likely continue to invite such analogies while staving off firm conclusions, thereby sustaining our fascination with them.

Although the scholarly community has largely shunned the Kirkendales' analogy (see especially Walker 1995), their musical observation about the six-part ricercar remains valid: Bach's keyboard fugues (i.e., those without an independent pedal line for the feet) are sometimes less forthcoming than his organ fugues, which tend to announce thematic entries with greater clarity. In the grandiloquent dance of the *Ricercar a 6*, six musical lines collaborate in close confines, sometimes in tandem and sometimes at cross purposes with one another; individual iterations of the one essential step (the royal theme) occasionally project from the whole but just as often are enveloped by it. The same kind of choreographic camouflage can be found elsewhere in Bach's keyboard music: the Fugue in F♯ minor from *WTC 1* has a couple of inverted subject entries that often escape notice. Such instances of artful concealment remind us of the myriad benefits of careful practice and quiet reflection.

A more functional explanation of the royal theme's various appearances in the *Ricercar a 6* might first acknowledge its status as a melody that serves (somewhat subversively in this hybrid piece) multiple purposes. Its official role, as fugue subject, determines the course of the initial exposition, but its subsequent segmentation in abundant ricercar-style writing subsumes bits and pieces of it in elaborate chains of imitative counterpoint—a daring move for a composer trying to make a good impression on a monarch who imposed a specific series of notes and expected a proper fugue, besides. Over the course of this monumental contrapuntal experiment, complete statements of the royal theme twice in each part counteract any potentially raised eyebrows, even if some of those entries are cleverly hidden. As intoned solemnly some twelve times, Frederick's theme becomes a cantus firmus in the manner of a medieval plainsong melody or a Lutheran chorale tune. By applying his considerable compositional expertise to the construction of an elaborate structure to house it, Bach showed in this curious fugue-cum-ricercar how to be subject to a theme while nevertheless seeking to adorn it.

## Gilding a Royal Melody

Seen in this way, the *Ricercar a 6* appropriates elements of another genre that was near and dear to this composer. Many chorale-based works from the Baroque era comprise comparable points of imitation, with motives derived from successive phrases of the melody appearing in "fore-imitation" at the head of (and sometimes throughout) each new section. In such a piece, the complete chorale melody usually sounds above or through the texture in a single voice, in long notes that may or may not be decorated and with each phrase segment punctuated by rests in that voice. In his *Ricercar a 6* Bach created comparable textures, with the royal theme coloring the contrapuntal fabric only occasionally, as do phrases of the hymn melody in a chorale fantasia. And yet, the royal theme roams freely in this piece in transposition, something one finds rarely in works based on a cantus firmus.

Bach employed cantus firmus technique in a more traditional manner in other works from the late 1730s and 1740s, including elaborate chorale settings in *Clavier-Übung III* and the "Confiteor" section of the *Symbolum Nicenum* portion of the Mass in B Minor.

Example 3.10  Contrapunctus 9, mm. 35–42 (soprano and tenor)

The primary theme of the *Art of Fugue* likewise impersonates a cantus firmus in several of that collection's compound fugues, in which it appears as a complement to subjects that have preceded it. This surprise manifests itself early in Contrapunctus 9, with an augmented version of the familiar tune ringing out at the top of a busy texture against this fugue's lithe initial subject, as Example 3.10 shows. This felicitous bit of invertible counterpoint reappears multiple times in this dazzling double fugue, giving all four voices a chance to "hold" the cantus firmus. Bach may have intended a similar effect in the final (missing) section of the unfinished fugue, with its three extant themes joined by the parent melody in a concluding section featuring four-part invertible counterpoint. A comparable combinatorial epiphany in late Bach occurs in *Musical Offering* toward the middle of the sonata's second movement (Example 3.11), when the royal theme appears suddenly against the leading idea of this *Allegro*—which, one realizes perhaps only belatedly, is itself a decorated variant of Frederick's melody.

In comparison, the *Musical Offering* canons explore systematically the royal theme's capacity for strict imitation of various kinds, some of which incorporate variants of Frederick's melody in canonic imitation while others deploy canonic voices against it. Bach engraved all but two of these concise contrapuntal wonders

**Example 3.11** Sonata from *Musical Offering*, Allegro (ii), mm. 46–53

in enigmatic notation, which omits the implied canonic voice. (Table 2.1 summarizes their distinct notational styles.) This traditional way to transmit a canon—also called *canon clausus* ("closed") or "puzzle" canon—marries a single line to be realized in multiple voices with clues that lead to a solution; additional non-canonic lines may also be involved. Titles or instructions sometimes specify the pitch level of the unnotated voice(s): at the unison or fifth, for example. (Renaissance music theorists considered this rule or instruction a "canon" in the legal or ecclesiastical sense, hence the etymology of the procedure or genre.) Of the ten canons in *Musical Offering*, several also feature contrapuntal devices like augmentation or inversion; one even mandates continuous modulation. Arranged sequentially in the original printing sections, these miniature musical riddles become steadily more demanding, with the final pair of canons obliging the player(s) to deduce the correct time and interval distance for the indicated canon.

Perhaps unsurprisingly for such a didactically minded composer, the five *Canones diversi super Thema Regium* (Figure 3.2) follow a progression comparable to that of the first seven contrapuncti from the *Art of Fugue*: from the simple to the complex. The former set begins with a *canzicrans* or "crab" canon, which mimics that animal's peculiar multi-directional skittering with simultaneous forward and backward movement. Bach indicated this operation in the traditional manner, with a single musical line whose initial

**Figure 3.2** Five *Canones Diversi* from *Musical Offering* (original edition, 1747)

time signature and clef are replicated at the end but upside down and backwards. To supply the canonic voice, a second player reads the original notation upside down, playing all notes from end to beginning. Realization by a solitary keyboard player is also possible, requiring only quick rescoring in two parts.

Despite the artifice—which is evident on the page—the aural result is an innocuous bit of counterpoint, with the canonic melody's long second half imposing a predictable harmonic sequence leavened only by a few well-placed syncopations. And yet in the act of playing, an adept practitioner might discover how Bach created this seemingly inscrutable musical crustacean. One invents first a complementary voice devoid of dissonance against the original melody, with no objectionable sonorities on strong beats. At that point, two mechanical tasks remain: swapping the position of both voices for the remainder then copying all notes in reverse order to verify a smooth result. Notation on two staves thereby becomes redundant; an upside-down clef at the end of a single composite line suffices. By this simple process, demystified by Marpurg in the *Abhandlung von der Fuge*, anyone who understands the basic rules of consonance and dissonance can devise a crab canon and notate it with similar concision.

The charming aural effect is akin to that of a bizarre echo chamber, one that returns to the source the original sound wave but in reverse order. Though such a wondrous machine had yet to be invented, mechanical automatons that attempted to replicate life itself were the rage in the middle of the eighteenth century: Jacques de Vaucason's "Digesting Duck," for example, whose ability to eat and defecate astounded many, including the educated elite. A comparably uncanny concoction, the first of Bach's *Canones diversi* functions as a kind of musical *amuse-bouche*—a crunchy bite that leads to more substantial canonic pleasures. It also shows how a cantus firmus may be set with perfect equanimity, in a non-hierarchical texture of two voices that share the same register and play identical material while starting at opposite ends. Circling around immediately to swap roles is part of the performance convention for such pieces, which may repeat in an endless self-contained loop.

The remaining four canons in this group are notated in two voices, with a third voice to be realized from instructions on the page. Two feature an unadorned royal cantus (Nos. 2 and 3) while the others decorate Frederick's melody (Nos. 4 and 5). Canon 2 uses the royal theme as a sturdy bass, above which two violins spar in stylish two-part strict imitation at the unison. As in the sonata, Bach provides specific instructions for instrumentation and detailed articulation marks, not just to enable but to shape performance. As Butler (2002b) has pointed out, this sonorous little marvel fits perfectly within Marpurg's galant canonic style; the unison canon causes the second player to be perceived as either echoing the first or supplying against it euphonious parallel thirds or sixths. With the artifice suitably masked, this canon bobs about, providing decorous counterpoint against the cantus firmus in the continuo. Butler wonders, as we might, whether such pieces—precisely because of their mixing of the archaic and the fashionable—appealed to progressive musicians of the 1740s and 1750s as a species of retro chic. Its swinging nature has continued to make converts far and wide, including the Modern Jazz Quartet, whose 1955 realization on vibraphone, piano, and double bass (as an introduction to "Softly, as in a Morning Sunrise" on their *Concorde* album) demonstrates that even learned counterpoint can be hip.

On the heels of this bit of exuberant play, the *Canon per Motum contrarium* (No. 3) channels a more introspective muse. With the royal theme now at the top of the texture, this canon's scalar *dux* descends while its *comes* ascends, from a starting pitch that must be determined by the player since the notation fails to indicate it. Contrary motion, in this case, produces thoroughly entwined canonic voices; the device also injects an occasional bit of awkwardness in momentary **false** (or "cross") **relations** (B♮ against B♭). In contrast to No. 2, where the royal theme activates and supports a lively canonic duet, this piece is a sonic abstraction, a musical mobile whose two primary elements (cantus firmus and canon) revolve around each other autonomously.

The canonic voices of No. 4 combine contrary motion and augmentation, with the royal theme transformed in the same manner as the primary variant of the main theme of the *Art of Fugue*: with passing tones and dotted rhythms (compare with Example 3.8a). On first encounter, doubled note values in the unnotated voice make this *Canon per Augmentationem, contrario Motu* harder to parse than Contrapunctus 7, whose (notated) augmented theme resounds through a dense surrounding texture. The problem in Bach's canon is partly registral: its imitative lines feint and parry around the embellished cantus firmus with no regard for social distancing. Sharp dotted figures and fast swooping scales bring tension and even uncertainty to the canonic voices, which can be resolved in multiple ways. The solution embraced by the Neue Bach Ausgabe (ed. Christoph Wolff) avoids extending the augmented voice beyond the point where it becomes problematic. Longer realizations, in which all eight bars of the *dux* are put into augmentation, require some ingenuity and high tolerance for cross relations. As Timothy Edwards (2010) and others have cautioned, the solution published by the Bach Gesellschaft (ed. Alfred Dörffel) stands at odds with the composer's usual practice in augmentation canons.

For the *Canon per Tonos*, the last of the *Canones diversi*, Bach loosened the C-minor moorings of the royal theme to divert it into an endlessly rising coil of counterpoint, with the entire texture climbing by whole tones with each repetition. A masterful trick, this "modulating canon" nevertheless sounds somewhat self-conscious, as if it has been sentenced to trudge perpetually up endless flights of stairs. Though weirdly cramped, it is nevertheless instructive. Both this canon and the second in the set provide the clearest evidence that Bach relied, when he could, on the most straightforward method for canonic composition: compose the first bar (or so) of the *dux*, copy it at the correct interval of imitation as the beginning of the *comes*, return to the *dux* to add more notes, and repeat until finished. When combined with a cantus firmus, this process assumes an additional layer of constraints, occasionally yielding melodies with little allure, as is certainly the case here. But the daring conceit of continuous modulation—with a royal theme, of all things, along for the ride—overrides any concerns about inelegant counterpoint. The only logical conclusion, on a lone unison, hardly provides satisfactory closure after such a heavily gilded and frankly disorienting journey.

"Resolving with canonic art" Frederick's idiosyncratic theme, as the inscription in the dedication copy puts it, these five canons illustrate with fittingly regal excess how even a melody with limited contrapuntal potential can still participate in a diverse array of strict procedures. Bach's concurrent work on the *Art of Fugue* had no such hindrance; few musical themes are better suited to adaptation and artifice. One wonders whether he pondered at length its shape before committing anything to paper. Or perhaps by this point in his career, as Emanuel Bach's letter to Forkel implies, the elder Bach grasped intuitively how to craft endlessly productive musical ideas. In either case, his last decade provided ample time to ponder and realize its potential while doing likewise in just a few weeks with a singular royal souvenir.

## SUGGESTIONS FOR FURTHER READING

In *The Keyboard Music of J. S. Bach* (2006), David Schulenberg authoritatively addresses compositional mechanics, original sources, and performance issues for both ricercari in *Musical Offering* and for the entire *Art of Fugue*. Hans T. David's *J. S. Bach's Musical Offering: History, Interpretation, and Analysis* (1945/72), although dated, offers thoroughgoing analyses of both ricercari; Donald Francis Tovey's detailed *Companion to The Art of Fugue* (1931) likewise remains an informative guide to musical processes in that collection. Of the many published discussions of individual movements in the latter work, some of the most perceptive may be found in Joseph Kerman, *The Art of Fugue: Bach's Fugues for Keyboard* (2005).

Among the many writings that propose interpretive strategies for these late contrapuntal collections, the most approachable include books on the *Art of Fugue* by Hans Heinrich Eggebrecht (1993) and Ewald Demeyere (2013). The former, as translated into English by Jeffrey Prater, argues for a spiritually infused conception of the whole, while the latter seeks to ground performance in contemporaneous music theory; Demeyere additionally offers in-depth readings of Contrapuncti 1–4. Penetrating criticism of this kind of scholarship, finally, may be found in Ruth HaCohen, "The Tonal, the Gestural, and the Allegorical in Bach's *Musical Offering*" (2006).

# 4

# Musical Gaming

With the *Art of Fugue* and *Musical Offering* Bach demonstrated, as we have seen, the capacity of related yet distinct themes to participate in multiple varieties of counterpoint, from the straightforward to the circular. The present chapter considers how both works also reflect the composer's longstanding attachment to a vigorous subculture of musical gaming, which in the eighteenth century encompassed everything from pithy puzzles requiring only a modicum of mechanical savvy to formidable tests of the most agile of minds and hands. This commitment can be seen in three overlapping areas, all examined in some detail here: the notational conventions of learned keyboard music, its potential for intellectual and performative stimulation, and its creative possibilities and limits.

## Visualizing Counterpoint

From their first appearance in printed form, Bach's *Musical Offering* and *Art of Fugue* have appealed principally to those with comprehensive musical training: *Kenner* (experts) rather than *Liebhaber* (amateurs), to borrow terms that appear frequently in eighteenth-century writing and music publishing. This target audience determined the look of both original editions, which mix enigmatic notation (most of the *Musical Offering* canons) with a set of instrumental parts (the sonata) and two distinct kinds of keyboard notation: open and keyboard score (the fugal pieces in both collections). The latter modes of notating music, which today

*Bach's* Art of Fugue *and* Musical Offering. Matthew Dirst, Oxford University Press.
© Oxford University Press 2024. DOI: 10.1093/oso/9780197536636.003.0005

tend to serve separate groups of practitioners, fostered in Bach's day distinct modes of interaction with musical sources. Open score, in which each individual voice or musical line appears on its own staff, complicates the reading process for a solitary keyboard player, who must assimilate and realize multiple lines at once. And yet, open score offers the clearest possible representation of individual voices in a polyphonic texture, as Bach himself demonstrated in the printed version of the *Ricercar a 6* and in all sources of the *Art of Fugue*. Bach's earlier keyboard collections, in contrast, all employ two-stave keyboard score, a more practical format for realization by two hands. Why the change for the *Ricercar a 6* in *Musical Offering* and for all the contrapuncti in the *Art of Fugue*? Bach's late turn toward open score in keyboard music suggests that he considered the benefits of this arrangement on the page more important than its inherent limitations.

He was hardly the first composer to make that distinction. In the early seventeenth century, the Roman virtuoso Girolamo Frescobaldi used the same two formats for multiple publications of his own music, which range from books of avant-garde toccatas (rhapsodic "touch" pieces) notated in keyboard score to collections of contrapuntal ricercari, canzonas, and capriccios in open score. With these volumes Frescobaldi amplified his reputation as an imaginative and daring yet scrupulously schooled player. Admired well beyond the Eternal City, Frescobaldi showed the world how to marry counterpoint and fantasy in keyboard works of various kinds. German musicians, as it turned out, were a particularly receptive audience.

Seventeenth-century German organists also adapted Netherlandish models to the needs of their confessional tradition. Samuel Scheidt, student of the great Dutch organist Jan Pieterszoon Sweelinck, played a comparable role to Frescobaldi in advancing an idiomatic keyboard style with a landmark publication of his own: the *Tabulatura Nova* (1624). Literally "new tablature," this three-volume set was novel in several ways. In sheer length and ambition, its expansive fantasies and chorale variations exceed even those of Sweelinck (which, by contemporary standards, are hardly short). Scheidt's keyboard monument was also the first to be published north of the Alps in the modern Italian format, with each line of music on its own staff. Musicians across Europe appreciated the layout of the *Tabulatura Nova*, even if German organists, Scheidt's primary audience, proved somewhat resistant to change; their beloved letter notation, also known as "keyboard tablature," endured through the turn of the century. (Bach himself reverted to this older practice multiple times for final measures at the bottom of an already full page.) As embraced by Scheidt in his *Tabulatura Nova* and by Frescobaldi in his *Fiori musicali* (1635), a copy of which eventually found its way into Bach's library, open score with modern clefs and notes became in the early Baroque the favored format for publications of the most rigorous keyboard works.

In a foreword to the *Tabulatura Nova*, Scheidt recommends transcribing its contents into tablature, by which means players determined for themselves how best to notate their favorite pieces. Frescobaldi, who could afford to be less accommodating, expected competent keyboardists to realize counterpoint in open score directly from the printed page, averring in the preface to *Fiori musicali* that this skill "distinguishes true *virtuose* from *ignoranti*." Bach's dedicatory preface to *Musical Offering* says nothing at all about the published format of the *Ricercar a 6*; and as far as we know, he never addressed notational matters for the *Art of Fugue*. He probably considered such explanations superfluous: in a preface to the 1752 print run of the latter work, Marpurg maintains that "the advantages of a good score have for a long time been incontestable." And indeed, those of us who play from keyboard score often keep full scores at hand for insight into the movement of individual voices and the relationships that obtain between them. The isolation of musical lines in separate staves is especially useful for clarifying (for the eye at least) multiple crisscrossing parts in the same register.

Tellingly, the other original source for the *Ricercar a 6*, which includes some revisions to the text of the engraved edition, is an autograph keyboard score that Bach made for his own use. The edition presents only the *Ricercar a 3* in the latter format, which reinforces visually its more casual treatment of Frederick's theme. Bach's *Musical Offering* followed, in other words, a historical distinction in notation as set forth in keyboard publications from the early seventeenth century. A single brace of two staves served for modish pieces while more traditional contrapuntal works, when published, occasionally appeared in open score, which obliges close study and perhaps transcription before playing.

Frescobaldi further commended his own keyboard music for performance on either organ or harpsichord, with discrete adjustments expected from one instrument to the next. This made sense of his equipment: the brilliant and limpid *ripieno* of the Italian Baroque organ adds color and sustain to this culture's crisp and assertive harpsichords. Bach's more diverse *instrumentarium* occasionally prompted explicit directives like *pedaliter* or *organo pleno*, but these are the exception rather than the rule. Title pages of some collections are deliberately vague: the "Klavier" in *Das wohltemperierte Klavier* refers to either clavichord or harpsichord. Others are more explicit: for Parts II and IV of the *Clavier-Übung*, Bach specified a two-manual harpsichord to accommodate *forte* and *piano* effects in the former plus complex hand crossings in the latter. The original editions of *Musical Offering* and the *Art of Fugue* are silent on this matter except for scoring indications in the former for its sonata (for transverse flute, violin, and continuo) and in two of its canons (one for the same trio configuration and the other for two violins plus continuo). Keyboard realization of the other movements is implicit from their notational style, as was the intended audience for both collections.

Devotees have always found much in them to savor, from esoteric recipes for infinite counterpoint to flashes of compositional and digital bravado; there's even a pair of gently disorienting musical mirrors. Approached in the right frame of mind and with sufficient knowledge, these works expand one's horizons through mental gymnastics akin to electronic gaming. The competitive spirit exemplified by their notation, as I argue below, also extends to their abstract design, web of allusions, and performative challenges.

## Endless Loops

The middle decades of the eighteenth century were a propitious time for virtuosos who could afford to publish their own music, thanks to a thriving culture of domestic keyboard playing across Europe. Prominent figures like Handel and C. P. E. Bach made the most of this opportunity with volumes of suites, sonatas, rondos, and other popular fare aimed principally at the burgeoning bourgeois audience. The comparatively modest print runs of Bach's *Clavier-Übung* volumes, which Peggy Daub (1996) and Andrew Talle (2008) have estimated at no more than a few hundred copies each, reflect a more rarefied kind of reception, one limited largely to industrious dilettantes and skilled professionals. Subsequent engraved editions of Bach's *Musical Offering* and the *Art of Fugue* allowed the composer and his heirs to share printed copies of these works with fellow members of Mizler's Society and to continue his lifelong exchange of musical gifts with circles of colleagues and friends—many of whom were, like Bach himself, aficionados of the learned arts.

This coterie cultivated canon, the most gnomic of musical genres, as a form of intellectual recreation. As traded among initiates, either in person or through correspondence, these sonic puzzles stimulated conversation and fostered the sharing of contrapuntal "secrets." This social aspect of canon can occasionally be gleaned from the sources themselves, including a Bach document that resurfaced in the early 1980s (discussed in Schieckel 1982). Within the pages of a family autograph album once owned by Johann Friedrich Mentz, professor of philosophy and poetry at the University of Leipzig during Bach's long tenure in that city, is a canon from Teodoro Riccio, who served as Kapellmeister in Ansbach around the turn of the seventeenth century, along with Bach's solution to the same. (The Germans once used autograph books as repositories for all manner of jottings, from signatures of friends and acquaintances to poems, small illustrations, and short pieces of music.) A single line of music with two clefs, each with its own key signature, shows clearly where each voice should begin, and a Latin inscription points the way toward resolution at the specified interval of the lower fifth: *Duo currebant simul. Et unus citius cucurrit* ("Two [voices] run simultaneously, one faster than the other"). Bach's facile solution, with doubled note values in the *comes*, required merely that he acknowledge both clefs and follow directions. No great miracle of counterpoint, the Riccio canon and Bach's realization were nevertheless preserved and inserted into Mentz's album as a memento of a shared pastime with a good friend.

Extant one-off canons from Bach's own hand span his career, from 1713 to 1749 (BWV 1072–1078 and 1086). Most were commemorative gifts for students, colleagues, and occasional visitors, with one offered in celebration of a new godchild, the son of Johann Gottfried Walther. Occasionally Bach's canons appeared in other media: the famous 1746 portrait by Elias Gottlieb Haußmann shows the composer tendering for the viewer's inspection a triple canon for six voices (BWV 1076), a veritable badge of musical erudition. (This same little gem was subsequently printed and distributed through Mizler's Society as Bach's initial gift to members.) Hardy nuggets of musical logic and redolent vestiges of convivial relationships with a network of like-minded enthusiasts, these single canons continue to engage, and the conversations they engender still require just a few intriguing notes on a page.

In collections incorporating multiple canons, Bach strove for maximum variety within parameters that differed from one project to another. *Musical Offering*, as we have seen, surveys the canonic subgenres with (among other things) a canon that moves simultaneously backwards and forwards and another that subjects a single line of music to a kind of time warp between voices moving at different rates of speed. The flashier *Art of Fugue* canons, in contrast, offer unpredictable shifts from one species of strict counterpoint to another. In both collections, Bach indicated canonic operations with descriptive titles, rubrics, and occasional cryptic messages, as was customary. Other markings specify stylistic manners or performance practices: dots and slurs make clear that Bach intended these pieces to be played, not just studied.

The original edition of *Musical Offering* presents all but one of its ten canons in enigmatic notation, with five crammed onto a single page (see Figure 3.2). Most can be played *ad infinitum* by following internal repeat signs, a conventional (though hardly prescriptive) feature of the genre. Less indulgent players may choose to stop at the end of a *dux-comes* cycle on either a unison, octave, open fifth, or some combination of those intervals. For canons that lack a strong closing gesture, such an ending may seem arbitrary or abrupt, the musical equivalent of hitting a brick wall. A more graceful conclusion to a perpetual canon often involves a short interpolation, whether composed or improvised: Bach's notated codas for the four canons in the *Art of Fugue* serve as useful models. Though he supplied nothing comparable for the canons in *Musical Offering*, an intrepid performer or editor may do so without violating the spirit of the genre.

In canon Bach relied, as did his contemporaries, on conventional signs and a terminology borrowed mostly from Latin, whose rarefied vocabulary restricted trade in this mode of musical play to those with a solid humanistic education. (For the educated classes of this era, rhetorical elaboration was second nature in a range of activities, from legal briefs to stage gestures.) In *Musical Offering* Bach extended this wordplay by mixing languages throughout its various printing units. The title page and preface (section one), along with the obligatory dedication to Frederick, are in German, notwithstanding the King's strong preference for French. The other four printing units incorporate Latin and occasionally Greek words for titles and rubrics of individual pieces plus an appropriately Italian heading for the characteristically Italianate *Sonata sopr' il Soggetto Reale* ("Sonata on the Royal Subject"); Bach added additional allegorical inscriptions in Latin to the copy sent to Frederick. While Latin may seem a strange choice for a corpus of keyboard and chamber pieces, the noble language of antiquity had long served in didactic sources to describe the mechanical devices of counterpoint, irrespective of genre.

Even if Bach's engravers decided the ultimate location of the canons in this collection, the order in which they appear in the original edition still suggests a graded pedagogical program. Taken together, the initial *Canon perpetuus super Thema Regium* (notated at the bottom of the final page of the *Ricercar a 3*) and the subsequent set of five *Canones diversi* comprise a sequence of increasingly intricate yet droll canons on the royal theme, all of which include either a discrete sign or a second clef to indicate the entry of the intended *comes*. Ignoring for the moment the *Fuga canonica* and the *Canon perpetuus [contrario motu]*, the final two canons (Figure 4.1) appear to be the most challenging of the lot, even for experienced musical gamers, who must solve them with little help from the composer.

The 1747 print supplies, seemingly for both, an oblique epigram derived from the Gospels: *Quarendo invenietis*. With these words, adapted from the Vulgate translation of the Sermon on the Mount (Matthew 7:7 and Luke 11:9), Bach recalled Jesus' promise to the faithful: "Ask and you will receive; seek and you will find; knock and the door will be opened." A bit of work, in other words, is required to solve this pair. The scriptural reference may also convey a larger theological message about the universality of sin and the gift of God's grace, as Marissen (1995) has proposed. In any case, Bach displayed impeccable manners by modifying the language of the

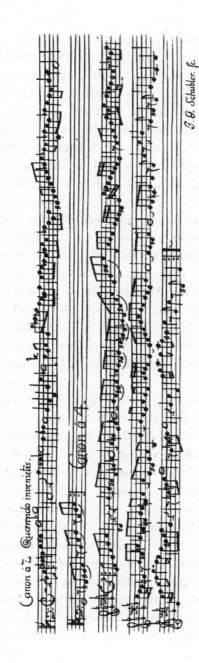

Figure 4.1 *Canon a 2* and *Canon a 4* from *Musical Offering* (original edition, 1747)

Vulgate, which expresses Jesus's message in the imperative *quaerite, et invenietis* ("Seek, and ye shall find"). As Anatoly Milka (2015/16) has pointed out, a king is not addressed in this manner, hence the gentler gerund in Bach's epigram, which becomes more invitation than admonishment: "In seeking you may find."

And be pleasantly surprised, the composer might have added. The *Canon a 2*, which adds chromatic passing tones and syncopations to the royal theme, explores melodic inversion in a subtly thoroughgoing way. Its single line sports two clefs, with an alto clef providing the *dux* and an upside-down bass clef yielding several inverted *comes* options. With no indication of a single "correct" relationship between voices, this canon allows for multiple solutions, as both Johann Friedrich Agricola and Johann Christoph Oley discovered in independent realizations made a few years after the work's initial publication. The *Canon a 4*, with a more flowing melody, is notated in a similar fashion, with a single line preceded by two clefs indicating the opening pitches for (in this case) four voices in canon at the unison and at the octave. Here, too, consumers of the first edition were expected to deduce subsequent points of entry.

Like the *Canon a 2*, the given melody of the *Canon a 4* alludes in broad outline to the royal theme, but its subsequent train is more than twice as long. Along with the *Ricercar a 6*, whose conclusion appears at the top of the same page in the original edition, this prodigious canon wants to be noticed. Its dizzying *dux* notwithstanding, a quick visual scan might prompt even a relative newcomer to match the repeated rhythmic figures of mm. 3–4 against similarly paired gestures in mm. 10–11 (and more in 17–18 and 24–25), thus solving the puzzle efficiently. More, in this case, came from less. Bach surely began his *Canon a 4* as a concise piece of fully invertible four-part counterpoint (an intricate harmonization, effectively, of the embellished royal theme) whose individual voices he then strung together into a single line. As such, the long and discursive melody commands attention on the page while sounding strangely confined in realization, in a revolving matrix whose individuated rhythms barely manage to keep the resulting counterpoint from sliding into chromatic queasiness. The decorated royal theme, in its final apotheosis, dominates the thick texture in virtually every bar, enacting through musical means the omnipotence of an absolutist ruler, as Yearsley (2002b) trenchantly observes. Indeed, Frederick's powerful shadow looms large here for the four players who dutifully pass his protracted melody back and forth, each awaiting their turn in a tightly circumscribed contrapuntal web.

There is, of course, a quieter option. Canon, by its very nature, may bring more satisfaction in one's imagination than in sounding form. This peculiar capacity of the genre, to transcend sonorities that would be shunned in less strict composition, has always encouraged enthusiasts to look beyond the notes themselves for insight into canon's meaning and significance. In its heyday, adherents compared themselves to magicians and even alchemists, who since antiquity had labored to transform humble materials into precious metals. From our vantage point, the masters of canon proved rather better at their own discipline's mumbo-jumbo, producing actual results (unlike their alloy-obsessed forebears) that could be shared and admired by peers and students. These learned occultists, whose activities Yearsley (2002a) has chronicled in detail, occasionally depicted their peculiar brand of sonic gold by embedding an enigmatic canon within an intricate visual web: a lavishly decorated cross or castle. Though practically minded writers on music railed against such arcana, which generally produced music of dubious value, its cult endured and continued to attract new followers, even after Bach's death.

Unsurprisingly, perpetual canons remain fertile ground for extra-musical allusion. Using analogies of all kinds, today's scholars rationalize such works—their order and number especially—and explain them via concepts borrowed from religion and theology, cosmology, even the occult. Most imaginative is Hans-Eberhard

Dentler's (2008) proposal that the perpetual canons in *Musical Offering* reflect the nine muses of Greek mythology and their related planets or stars, with the Canonic Fugue representing Earth. Dentler's thesis relies on a larger agenda he posits for the entire collection, whose fascicles he sees as somehow exemplifying Boethius's three general categories of music; the canons, he argues, were inspired by Johannes Kepler's description of the heavenly spheres (in his *Weltharmonik* of 1619), as filtered through the writings of Andreas Werkmeister and thence to Bach. More theologically minded scholars consider all ten canons (including the Canonic Fugue) a numerical allusion to Old Testament law, made concrete in the Ten Commandments. The dispersal of the canons throughout the various fascicles of the original edition, though potentially an argument against this comparison (Moses brought the commandments down the mountain as one contiguous set, after all), may be explained as a practical decision on the part of the engravers: to fill empty space on the pages of the various printing units.

Though such descriptions may tax the reader's comfort level with disparate comparison or philosophical paradox, they are often thought-provoking and occasionally enlightening. A sacralized *Musical Offering* gains support from numerous groups of ten elsewhere in the repertoire. By the late 1740s, Bach had repeatedly summoned biblical law, as articulated in both the Old and New Testaments, in texted and untexted works. Of the two organ settings of *Dies sind die heil'gen zehn Gebot* ("These are the Holy Ten Commands") in *Clavier-Übung III*, the first (BWV 678) treats the five primary phrases of the chorale melody canonically in two parts ($5 \times 2 = 10$), while the second (BWV 679), a manuals-only *fughetta*, includes precisely ten entries of a subject based on the same tune. The opening chorus of Cantata 77 likewise incorporates ten distinct entries of this chorale melody, delivered on a solo trumpet above a busy texture of strings and voices and a continuo line that supplies a canon in augmentation against five of the trumpet's phrases. Between those ten canonic pillars, the chorus declaims the Greatest Commandment, in which Jesus urges the Pharisees to

"Love the Lord your God with all your heart . . . and your neighbor as yourself."

It hardly matters whether anyone perceives, in performance, the theological significance of such things; the allusion is clear in the notes themselves. The prevalence of similar groups of ten in comparable sacred works by other composers leaves no doubt about this number's extra-musical meaning for those who provided music for the Christian liturgy. Whether it retained that meaning in a corpus of keyboard and chamber music remains an open question, however. Adherents of the German Enlightenment had little use for allegories premised entirely on counting, even as such things continued to appeal to orthodox Lutherans and members of didactically minded circles like Mizler's Society. At best, the ten canons in Bach's *Musical Offering* may have delivered a veiled message to the Potsdam court: to remind Frederick, whose nominal Calvinism was tempered by a strong suspicion of all things religious, of the one power greater than his own. Additional support for this kind of argument may be found elsewhere; multiple musical sources pair *Qui se humiliat exaltabitur* ("Whoever humbles himself shall be exalted") with canons in contrary motion. But with intellectual and spiritual messages routinely commingled in canon during this era, singular meanings likely had limited value for experienced musical gamers.

As the foregoing demonstrates, canon in Bach's day appealed primarily to musicians whose knowledge of counterpoint was accompanied by significant learning in other fields, including philosophy and religion. For this discerning community, canon functioned as a genial pastime, one whose manifold challenges could stimulate the mind and eye as well as the ear. Frederick the Great may not have been an official member of this club, but he was surely familiar with the basic rules of the game; the occasional presence of learned devices like stretto in his own chamber works suggests a healthy respect for traditional modes of musical discourse. Quite a few German composers, even those who excelled in opera and other more popular genres, trafficked in such music: Telemann in his *Canons mélodieux* (1738), for example. What Frederick made of the ten canons in *Musical Offering* is not for us to know, however, despite Bach's efforts to engage him in the dedication copy.

To wit, the margin of No. 4 in the *Canones diversi* carries this bit of royal flattery: "As the notes grow, so may the fortunes of the King" (*Notus crescentibus crescat Fortuna Regis*). This canon's principal device, augmentation of note values in imitation, thereby acquires allegorical significance: growth is preordained, as is Frederick's glorious destiny. The fifth canon of the same set, devised to modulate steadily upwards through the octave as the canon repeats multiple times, bears a similarly ingratiating inscription: "As the modulation rises, so does the King's glory" (*Ascendenteque Modulatione ascendat Gloria Regit*). This perpetually proving bit of contrapuntal dough suggests something else entirely to Douglas Hofstadter (1979), who compares it to M. C. Escher's fanciful depictions of closed loops via conjoined staircases or waterfalls without issue. Like Escher's visual conundrums, Bach's canon takes a considerable journey only to arrive precisely where it started. Is the joke on those who realize this only late in the game?

## What Rules?

Canon can also generate vigorous chamber pieces or virtuoso showstoppers, as Bach shows elsewhere in *Musical Offering* and in the *Art of Fugue* especially. The former collection's *Fuga canonica*, to address briefly this curious hybrid, combines elements of canon and fugue in the manner of an artifice-laden sonata movement for unspecified forces: either two treble instruments plus bass or a single treble instrument plus keyboard, in which case the latter covers two parts. Notated in two voices, its solution requires minimal expertise. Two clefs on the top line plus a symbol for the entry of the *comes* make realization of the second (unnotated) treble part a straightforward matter. Over an independent bass line well suited to continuo realization, the canonic voices repeat the royal theme several times and on different scale degrees, in the manner of a fugue subject, while staying in exact canon throughout. Just before the end, the royal theme migrates—out of the blue—to the bass for a last statement in the tonic key. A coda ensues, with just enough free counterpoint to supply definitive closure for all three voices.

In the fully-scored *Canon perpetuus* that follows the Sonata in the original edition and calls for the same group of players, Bach realized his own canonic challenge—a decorated royal theme and its inversion set against each other above a continuo line—with two equally good solutions that run contiguously. At the outset, the flute plays the recto theme with the violin answering in inversion. Once this canon has run its course (at m. 18 in the top part), a contrapuntal rearrangement or *evolutio* follows directly, with the flute still in the lead but now in inversion to the violin's recto reply. The clever exchange of direction between *dux* and *comes*, underlined by modulation to the dominant, makes for another kind of generic crossbreed: a canon masquerading as a chamber trio. Perhaps Bach took inspiration here from Telemann's canonic duet sonatas of just a few years before.

More daunting for performers is the central trio sonata in *Musical Offering*, which follows a conventional formal plan: the *sonata da chiesa* or "church sonata" for two treble instruments plus basso continuo, as crystallized by Arcangelo Corelli and embraced by everyone in the years surrounding 1700. Like many such works, Bach's four-movement sequence comprises (in order) a sober Largo, a fugal Allegro, a languorous Andante, and a gigue-like concluding Allegro; its surface textures and underlying logic are, however, uniquely Bachian. Its inclusion in *Musical Offering* is similarly idiosyncratic: contemporaneous publications rarely mingled chamber with keyboard music. Obligation, it would seem, occasionally trumped norms in music publishing.

Having written few sonatas in this standard format, Bach duly
produced one for the royal instrument while making room for the
royal theme in various guises. The triadic beginning of Frederick's
melody may have prompted the opening movement's throbbing
continuo line (mm. 1–4) and the primary theme of the ensuing
Allegro, as many have noted. Of greater consequence is the latter
movement's most famous moment: after more than forty bars of
energetic counterpoint, Frederick's melody makes a sonorous entrance in the bass (see Example 3.11), from which it eventually
migrates (at the *da capo*) to the flute, thereby demonstrating the
invertibility of both themes in double counterpoint. Bach's closing
movement, in turn, subjects the royal theme to a lively dance that
accelerates, bit by bit, into wild carousel of swirling motives and
churning harmonies. In this Allegro and in the preceding Andante
especially (to which we shall return in Chapter 5), one senses an
effort to impress, mostly with excess. Doing so in the context of a
sonata, one of the most popular of musical genres at mid-century,
may have raised a few eyebrows but was entirely in keeping with
this composer's habitual willfulness with stylistic norms.

The four canons in the *Art of Fugue* aspire to similar heights but
within a more rarefied species of musical composition. Providing
textural contrast to the contrapuncti within a comparable overall
trajectory of increasing complexity, these two-part wonders illustrate the most rigorous connotation of the *fuga* principle. As with
the whole, Bach tinkered with these canons over a period of several
years, at some point abandoning single-line notation since it could
accommodate the final form of only the *Canon alla Ottava*. The end
results, like the four *Duetti* in *Clavier-Übung III*, are strangely protracted duos that give musical gamers much to ponder. Detailed
titles indicate their respective operations, which in three of four
canons include two contrapuntal devices: the *Canon alla Decima
[in] Contrapunto alla Terza*, for instance, specifies canon at the
tenth and invertible counterpoint at the third (or tenth). All are,
properly speaking, composite works that eventually incorporate either melodic or contrapuntal inversion of their initial material.

In the Canon at the Octave, whose triplet-infused melody is a sprightly variant of the inverted parent theme, Bach highlights the beginnings of multiple internal canons by inserting rests before new entries, which include a tonal *dux* from m. 25 and a real inversion from m. 41. Similar junctures in the other three canons are either elided or cleverly concealed; Bach shows only in the first what to look for in the others, and surprises lurk throughout. In the Canon at the Twelfth, sudden imitation at the octave at m. 34 with a radically reduced distance between *dux* and *comes* (two beats here, as opposed to eight bars at the beginning) proves deceptive in the next measure, and the pretense of this interior canon quickly falls apart. Eight bars later, with the left-hand entry of a proper *comes* but at the octave instead of the twelfth, Bach's sleight-of-hand becomes retrospectively apparent: the right hand, which had been following the left, has taken the lead. Even experts may miss the clue in the itemized title, which specifies both canon at the twelfth and invertible counterpoint at the fifth (or twelfth). The light dawns only on reflection: the latter operation—by which means a twelfth becomes a unison, an eleventh becomes a second, etc.—yields canon at the octave. Following this deft *evolutio*, an equally sneaky return to the opening material begins with a brief bit of close imitation at the octave (mm. 66–67), which threatens to obscure the return of the initial *dux* in the left hand (at m. 68). The counterpoint gives the impression of seamlessness, though one senses in the act of playing that something isn't quite right, and that's part of the fun.

Bach indulged such bravura demonstrations of contrapuntal fusion repeatedly during his last years: in the longest of the Canonic Variations on *Vom Himmel hoch* and in the second *Canon perpetuus* from *Musical Offering*, as noted above. But in the *Art of Fugue* he went one step further, with canons whose notes occasionally seem to be generating themselves, the relentless imitation imposing its will somehow on both composer and player. Tempering the mechanical in these pieces are articulation marks and occasional embellishments that extract expressive gestures from otherwise dogged lines. But even here, the performative layer sometimes serves only to reinforce the impression left by an inscrutable series of notes: the long slurs in the Augmentation Canon's chromatic passagework render this angular, almost jeering canon—premised, as Tovey sneers, on an "uncouth *canto fermo*"—audibly wobbly in several places. More than any other examples of the genre, from Bach or anyone else, these canons "dramatize the tension between thinking and playing, between reflection and action," as Yearsley (2002b) puts it.

Their extreme demands place these canons in a special class, even for Bach. Hand crossings turn up occasionally: most prominently, at the end of the Canon at the Octave, where the player's right hand must nail a sudden toss to the bottom of the keyboard. In the Canon at the Tenth, Bach made room at the final cadence for something he normally eschewed in notated counterpoint: an opportunity for extemporization (see Example 4.1). The "finale" portion of this curiously bipolar canon, which combines a solemn subject with extravagant elaboration, speeds up the entry of the inverted theme in the bass while slowing down the treble, destabilizing what had been a leisurely if intricate duet dominated by the swaying rhythms of triplets and sextuplets. Bach pairs this startling thematic entry, which subjects the prevailing syncopation to diminution, with a rhapsodic right-hand part that shoots upwards only to land on an open fourth against the left hand at the penultimate bar line. Fermatas in both parts plus the directive "cadenza" in the original edition mandate an improvised conclusion. Experienced players—especially those schooled on the contemporaneous sonata repertoire, which gives occasional opportunities

**Example 4.1** *Canon alla Decima*, mm. 79–82

for extemporization—might append a new imitative idea or adapt one from earlier in the work, thereby expanding Bach's abrupt finale; there's certainly plenty of pent-up energy to dispel. Or has the composer set a trap here for overconfident performers? One cannot hope to win such a contest against the likes of Sebastian Bach, although one might read the invitation differently—as a sign of the "unbreachable rift" between the mechanical and the spontaneous, as Yearsley (2002c) proposes.

A more mundane explanation for this anomalous moment may be adduced as well. Butler (2008) has shown conclusively that the composer himself prepared the printer's copy of all four canons; the engravers, in turn, followed Bach's lead on matters of notation and pagination. Of the four, only the Canon at the Tenth extends to the very edges of both its pages, one consequence of which is the lack of room for a decorative cartouche like those that grace left-over space after the final cadences of the other three canons and the pages of several of the contrapuncti. Here, by contrast, Bach and his engravers barely had room for the double bar; even a brief curlicue was out of the question. Might the cadenza be a quick punt on Bach's part, one motivated (at least in part) by the lack of room for additional counterpoint? Approached in this spirit, the obligatory cadenza seems less a thrown gauntlet than an invitation for further play.

For those engaged with the whole work, this opportunity for a bit of summary improvisation may recall similar moments late in Contrapuncti 1, 6, and 13, where Bach elongates, by means of either rests or fermatas, rhetorically charged chords. In the most directly comparable of these, the first fugue stops dead in its tracks on the heels of its most impassioned sequence (see Example 3.2). Instead of resolution, long rests isolate a subsequent tonic chord in second inversion, the conventional invitation for a cadenza, but neither the autograph nor the first edition gives an explicit directive, as in the Canon at the Tenth. Attempts to embellish this carefully groomed aporia in the first fugue, to borrow Joseph Kerman's (2005) term and his argument, risk prettifying a powerful void, just as added cadenzas would do in the "9/8" Prelude and Fugue in C major for organ (BWV 547), both halves of which build to a climax of sonorous chords punctuated by rests. In the opening colloquy of his treatise on counterpoint and fugue, perhaps Bach intended to point beyond the moment—as Purcell did with halting choral diction at the end of *Dido and Aeneas* ("never, never part")—so that we may contemplate what lies ahead. Silence, in such a reading, focuses the mind.

Ultimately, such choices rely on individual judgment about the implications or even the worth of a particular passage. Elsewhere in the *Art of Fugue*, Kerman proposes to shorten a notorious bridge between the first and second sections of Contrapunctus 10, thereby eliminating some "crude and unlovely" lower voices. We may be tempted to do likewise, and for good reason: to improve a fugue that Bach himself revised at least once. Its early version, No. 6 in the autograph, begins with a laidback treble entry of the dotted-note variant of the inverted main theme, just as in Contrapunctus 5 but an octave higher. For Contrapunctus 10 Bach added a new introductory section that explores the imitative potential of what had been a countersubject in the original fugue. In so doing, he transferred that fugue's opening exposition to m. 23 of Contrapunctus 10 and added new counterpoint to accompany the initial subject up to its corresponding answer (at m. 26).

In context, the enhanced texture of mm. 23–26—comprising a suddenly athletic bass line and a curiously abbreviated alto entry that anticipates the (actual) answer in the tenor a few bars later—sounds like artful camouflage; though well intended, this passage inevitably come across as just so much contrapuntal glue. (Kerman's suggested elision, despite its tasteful rewriting of mm. 22 and 26, proves equally problematic by excising the subject entry at m. 23, whose slight overlap with the tenor answer is reproduced a few bars later in a bass and alto pairing. The missing subject would be sorely missed: a fugal exposition in four voices, even for a headstrong composer like Sebastian Bach, assumes four successive entries of the theme.) At the very least, and notwithstanding the inelegant seam, the multiple extant versions of Contrapunctus 10 show us that fugues on multiple subjects are sometimes composed one section at a time, and not always from beginning to end.

The early version's leisurely exploration of the *Art of Fugue* theme *a 4*, to pick up where we left off, leads to a series of subject entries accompanied by a peculiar countersubject comprising a pair of mirrored quarter-note motives plus a rising scale in eighth notes (Example 4.2). A kind of anti-melody, it nevertheless proves a dexterous partner for the primary theme in counterpoint at the tenth and at the octave. Sometime after completing this first version of the fugue, Bach realized that his unprepossessing countersubject could also generate an exposition on its own, hence the new beginning for Contrapunctus 10, replete with stretti and inverted entries. His addition transformed a fugue with a consistent though late arriving countersubject into a compound (or double) fugue on two subjects, which in turn yielded for the engraved edition a pair of comparable fugues: Contrapuncti 9 and 10 both begin with idiosyncratic themes that are eventually combined with the main theme of the whole.

**Example 4.2** Contrapunctus 10, mm. 44–48 (alto and tenor)

Within this common frame Bach sought maximum variety between double fugues by treating the parent melody's appearance in distinct ways. In Contrapunctus 9, which lacks strongly defined sections, we hear the main theme unambiguously and repeatedly (from m. 35 onwards) as a slow-moving cantus firmus against this fugue's buoyant initial subject (see Example 3.10). The published version of Contrapunctus 10, in contrast, devotes a second exposition to the *Art of Fugue* theme before combining it, as Example 4.2 illustrates, with this fugue's enigmatic initial melody. The juxtaposition of both themes (worked out in the early version as interplay of subject and countersubject, respectively) produces an increasingly dramatic series of combinations, the last four of which feature two voices sounding simultaneously the same theme in parallel thirds or sixths. Such variety is to be expected in compound fugue, which generally has a more variegated fabric than counter- or stretto fugues that fixate on a single subject, hence Bach's openness to an entirely new section. The incongruities of Contrapunctus 10 may explain why his posthumous editors included both versions of this fugue in the original edition; comparative study offers significant insight into this "strange composite work of rare beauty," as Kerman lovingly describes it. For those who choose to engage, this double fugue encourages a substantially different kind of response from that elicited by Canon at the Tenth: the canon's cadenza obliges invention, while the fugue elicits criticism.

## Looking-Glass Counterpoint

Fugues with three themes demonstrate similar flexibility in overall design. Book 1 of the *WTC* includes two examples of the most concise option, with a subject and two consistent countersubjects: the Fugues in C minor and B♭ major. Triple invertible counterpoint, which also generates the Prelude in A major from the same collection, typically provides the basic architecture for such pieces in various rotations of three mutually combinatorial ideas. In comparison, a compound fugue with three themes may favor only the first melody with an independent exposition, as happens in the Fugue in C♯ minor from *WTC 1*, in which a second and third theme appear in a second section with no internal division. A compound fugue may also treat all three themes independently before combining them, as happens in the Fugue in F♯ minor from *WTC 2*. A tripartite fugue does not oblige triple invertible counterpoint, however, as demonstrated in the "St Anne" organ fugue (BWV 552/2), whose second and third themes do not combine with each other.

Contrapunctus 8 and Contrapunctus 11, the two triple fugues in the *Art of Fugue,* are likewise compound fugues on three subjects in multiple sections but with a peculiar twist: their shared themes are reordered, inverted, and otherwise transformed from one fugue to the other. In his fair copy of what became the *Art of Fugue,* Bach placed these fugues next to each other, thereby highlighting their extraordinary nature as *alio modo* renderings of the same material, one *a 3* and the other *a 4.* The 1751/52 edition, in contrast, situates them at opposite ends of a group of four compound fugues, perhaps to establish symmetry via their respective number of subjects (3-2-2-3) or to improve page turns.

Contrapunctus 8, with three voices, begins with a loping yet mostly scalar melody (Example 4.3a) whose gradual descent of an octave is interrupted by a couple of upward leaps of a fourth. A long trill settles things by restoring the drive toward bottom D, after which a leap up the octave for a slurred series of three step-wise quarter notes, repeated in the next bar, provides an expressive overlap with the fugal answer. Anyone proceeding linearly through the collection may be puzzled by this subject, especially after seven fugues permeated by the *Art of Fugue* main theme; and yet, it retains at least a few vestiges of the parent melody, from shared chromaticism to the strong articulation of D minor in both. After thirty bars of exploration, a pedal point prompts what sounds like a final statement of this new theme in the bass and a firm cadence, stylishly inflected with appoggiaturas in the upper parts. An additional

Example 4.3  (a) Contrapunctus 8, mm. 1–7; (b) mm. 39–42

compositional element then appears: a quicker, more insistent secondary subject (Example 4.3b), whose repeating cross-stitched
motive allows for considerable flexibility in subsequent iterations.
Its suspended dissonances against the first theme, previewed in the
latter's penultimate entry in the previous section (m. 28), color both
triple fugues to an extraordinary degree.

The next juncture in Contrapunctus 8, heralded in mm. 90–92
with a conspicuous burst of rhythmic activity in the bass, ends on
a half-cadence that tees up the third and final subject: the inverted
original theme now transformed—as if by Brahms, Tovey muses—
into an ostinato whose most prominent feature is a recurring rest
on downbeats (Example 4.4a). Three closely spaced statements
(from m. 94 onwards) celebrate the return of this old friend before
yielding to a long pedal below the first two themes and a subsequent return to quick motion in the bass, both of which signal an
impending cadence (m. 124). Bach begins the fourth and final section of this sinewy fugue directly, with a sonorous pair of simultaneous entries of the first theme in two lower voices against the
second theme above. One more combination of both themes lands
on A minor (m. 135) before segueing into a lengthy episode. After
nearly a dozen bars, a swell of chromatic eighth-note passagework
in contrary motion announces the long-anticipated combination of
all three themes, which begins halfway through m. 147 (Example
4.5). Multiple rotations of this complex follow, and there's even one
last virtuosic riff, this time in the topmost voice. As the dust settles,
a final combination in the home key brings the all-important

**Example 4.4** (a) Contrapunctus 8, mm. 94–98 (alto only);
(b) Contrapunctus 11, mm. 1–5

**Example 4.5**  Contrapunctus 8, mm. 147–152

ostinato theme to the bass, where it resolves—for the first and only time—to the tonic note.

Bach's autograph continues with a mirrored reflection of the very same theme (Example 4.4b) at the start of the companion triple fugue, which in the edition appears as Contrapunctus 11. On its own, this new iteration recalls the basic shape of the parent theme, albeit within the ostinato pattern first suggested by the tail of the initial subject of Contrapunctus 8 and fully realized in that fugue's final subject in inverted form. Bach gives this melody a comparatively tight exposition in Contrapunctus 11, with no filler between the obligatory entries and just one additional subject statement (from m. 22). The latter's syncopated harmonization and its drive toward cadential resolution leave little doubt that this theme has, for the moment, run its course.

A second section features the initial theme from Contrapunctus 8, now turned on its head (Example 4.6). To accompany this awkward-sounding inversion, Bach settled on a series of quarter

**Example 4.6**  Contrapunctus 11, mm. 27–30

notes trooping up a fifth by half steps, an ungainly progression rarely seen in music of any era. The latter motive, which attracts considerable attention, effectively masks the solecisms of its contrapuntal partner; it also comes to dominate the texture in ascending and descending scales that expand to fill the octave (mm. 44–47 in the tenor) and inspire migrating chains of parallel sixths and thirds (mm. 64–69). It behaves, in other words, more like a subject than a countersubject, thereby increasing the rhetorical temperature of this fugue through abundant chromaticism.

A few dozen bars into this section, a striking ascent in the soprano and an equally memorable descent in both soprano and bass (mm. 52–57) nearly obscure a surprise: an inversion of the initial subject/countersubject complex (from m. 27) at mm. 57–58. Cleverly, a prominent appoggiatura (at the downbeat of m. 57) cloaks this reprise by borrowing the second subject's first two notes for the end of the previous phrase; once again, we realize only belatedly what's happened and admire in hindsight Bach's remarkable ingenuity. The return brings no relief from the constantly churning harmonies, however, which intensify before finally collapsing at m. 71 into A minor, at which point the first subject of this fugue returns, once again turned upside down. As if exhausted, the accompanying parts sigh a few times (with indicated appoggiaturas driving this feeling home) before regaining strength for a few more entries and a stronger cadence at m. 89 in the relative major.

A third theme, an extended inversion of the second subject of Contrapunctus 8, then joins the party with its partner from the earlier fugue and, eventually, that subject's new chromatic-scale pendant. The incessant eighth-note idea eventually crowds out the others for a powerful series of four simultaneous entries at m. 130, in both recto and inverted forms (Example 4.7). Lurking in the harmonic background from m. 129 onwards is a dominant pedal A, which reasserts itself twice before finally cadencing in m. 146 to C, of all places, where a thematic entry must compete once again with a cadential figure for attention, thus blunting the former's impact. The harmonic shock also upstages a key moment in Contrapunctus

**Example 4.7**  Contrapunctus 11, mm. 129–132

11: the combination of all three themes in invertible counterpoint
(Example 4.8). Here the advantage of open score is undeniable,
since one sees on the page what might otherwise go unnoticed.

**Example 4.8**  Contrapunctus 11, mm. 145–148

Bach's final cards trump even that maneuver. Arguably the most
stunning juxtaposition in this fugue occurs in mm. 158 and 164,
where the ostinato variant of the parent theme rings out in simultaneous recto and inverted entries in double counterpoint at the
octave, then at the tenth, recalling the grand conclusion to the
Fugue in B♭ minor from *WTC 2*, where all four voices participate
in hyper-stretto in opposite directions. One final combination of
all three themes follows (from the last beat of m. 174), with the soprano hitching a ride upwards in parallel motion with the most active of these. A craggy chromatic descent in all voices prepares one
last entry of the ostinato-like main theme, which sings out trium-
phantly in the top voice, in mirrored opposition to its position at the
end of Contrapunctus 8. Like its partner piece, this immense fugue
with three subjects also comes to rest with the *Art of Fugue* main
theme finally resolving to the tonic note. Delayed gratification, one

of Bach's favorite musical strategies, is achieved here through a singular coincidence of melodic and harmonic goals.

With long-sought closure finally achieved in a group of four highly discursive compound fugues, the original edition turns next to more rigorously mirrored kinds of counterpoint. Within the reflective frame of mirror fugue, Contrapunctus 12 proffers a dose of stile antico serenity and Contrapunctus 13 a spry dance. This rarely encountered subgenre poses some unusual compositional demands: one must contemplate, for example, each recto interval against its inverted corollary. To complicate matters further, certain harmonic progressions change character when inverted, with dominant becoming subdominant and vice versa. The constant obligation to dual functionality imposes a noticeably restrained harmonic language on Contrapunctus 12, whose four voices exhibit none of the daring chromaticism of the previous fugues. In Contrapunctus 13, with one fewer voice to manage, Bach could afford to be more adventuresome.

In his fair copy, Bach notated these fugues synoptically, rendering on each page recto and inverted iterations as mirror images of each other (Figure 4.2). For the engraved edition, the composer and

**Figure 4.2**  Beginning of Contrapunctus 12 from Bach's autograph manuscript of the *Art of Fugue*

his publisher abandoned this arresting visual arrangement (probably to ensure that all four items fit neatly onto two-page openings) and doubled all note values, giving the former fugue especially an archaic appearance. The transfer from visibly mirrored autograph to separately paginated engraving plates evidently caused some confusion for Bach's heirs and engravers about the internal order of items. Though he left in the autograph neither rubrics nor titles for either mirror fugue, Bach surely notated *rectus* above *inversus*, since we generally read down, not up, the page. (Alternatively, one might question whether a mirror fugue comprises an original and its reflection or rather two inverted opposites. In any case, the Schmeider catalogue follows the autograph's order, with the top items as BWV 1080/12/1 and 13/1 and the bottom items as BWV 1080/12/2 and 13/2, respectively.) In contrast, the 1751/52 edition presents both iterations of each fugue in the opposite order, with both portions of Contrapunctus 12 labeled *inversus*, a word that may indicate only that they are inversions of each other; the recto iteration of Contrapunctus 13 is titled in the same incorrect manner. Several otherwise reliable modern editions, in stubborn solidarity with the engraved print, perpetuate the latter mistake, for which Butler (2008) has advanced a good explanation: Bach seems not have prepared the engraver's template of the actual *inversus* portion of Contrapunctus 13 (BWV 1080/13/2). Advancing illness may have also prevented careful proofing of the original edition. (See Chapter 2 of the present study for a brief catalogue of its other missteps.)

For Contrapunctus 12 Bach revisited the vocal texture of the Fugues in B♭ minor from both books of the *WTC*, whose individual lines move with a similar deliberateness and sense of purpose. And yet, his mirror fugue eschews the habitual rigor of stile antico counterpoint. During its initial exposition, perhaps the only place in fugue where one assumes absolute independence of the parts, voices begin to pair off into sonorous duets: mellifluous chains of thirds and sixths (which invert beautifully) permeate the texture in

**Example 4.9** (a) Contrapunctus 12 *rectus*, mm. 1–5;
(b) Contrapunctus 13 *rectus*, mm. 1–5

virtually every bar, to the extent that one loses track of the subject itself (Example 4.9a), an elegant triple-time adaptation of the parent theme. Once introduced, this subject quickly becomes submerged in scalar figuration adapted from the retiring quarter notes that have long been lurking at its end. As a result, nothing seems to happen—by design—in this fugue. Its wondrously narcoleptic effect bores many writers, who fail to appreciate the irony of a fugue so uninterested in propagating its own subject. When inverted, this piece loses none of its queer charm, though certain gestures like the final decoration sound anomalous either way. As with Alice's looking glass, the mirror may serve a metaphorical purpose here, as the game acquires new and not entirely flattering rules.

The chipper subject of the second mirrored pair (Example 4.9b), with its bold leaps and flowing triplets, brightens the mood considerably. Since an exact mirror image would oblige the middle voice to remain in place as a pivot, Bach instead exchanged the positions of all three voices for the inversion. Effectively a rotating counter-fugue, Contrapunctus 13 also mixes recto and inverted forms of its subject throughout both iterations. Frequent one-bar sequences impose a gently thumping harmonic rhythm under the counterpoint, while a rhetorical pause on a diminished seventh chord, smartly placed a dozen bars before the final cadence, injects an additional bit of playfulness. Bach eventually expanded both iterations of this mirror fugue into a pair of pieces for two keyboards, both of which include a fourth non-imitative voice. Whether he meant for this arrangement to be published as part of the *Art of Fugue* remains unclear, however. Perhaps he hoped it would inspire re-scorings of other movements in the work, thus providing yet another opportunity for interactive engagement. In any case, the arrangement assists players challenged by the original, which occasionally imposes parallel tenths on a single hand. Curiously, Bach left no comparable arrangement of Contrapunctus 12, despite similar stretches.

Though not bound by strict imitation internally, both mirror fugues commandeer certain elements of the canonic arsenal. Their unusual digital demands invite transcription as keyboard duets (as Bach himself demonstrated) or as chamber music, the two customary ways of realizing puzzle canons in three or more parts. Their shared "party trick" of complete melodic invertibility manifests itself occasionally in canon (e.g., the *Canon a 2* from *Musical Offering*) but rarely in fugue; even Marpurg avoids discussing this exotic subgenre, referring readers of the *Abhandlung von der Fuge* to consult the *Art of Fugue* instead. As more recent writers have observed, Bach may have taken his cue from Dieterich Buxtehude's *Mit Fried und Freud ich fahr' dahin* (BuxWV 76), which comprises two short pairs of pieces, one in quadruple invertible counterpoint and the other a four-part mirror inversion. Buxtehude created these miniature marvels (each labeled *contrapunctus* and *evolutio*, respectively) for a 1671 funeral service and published them in open score three years later. Whether or not Bach knew them, by the 1740s he had plenty of experience with melodic inversion in three-part contrapuntal textures, including the concluding gigues of the sixth "English" Suite and the third and sixth of the Partitas in *Clavier-Übung I*. In all three of these binary-form dances, Bach recapitulates at the beginning of the second half his initial contrapuntal entries as mirrored inversions, with varying degrees of intervallic adjustment from one to the other.

Gazing deeply into the reflective depths of Contrapuncti 12 and 13, Hans Heinrich Eggebrecht (1984/93) finds in these pieces the revelation of God's grace, after the all-too-human struggle of Contrapunctus 11. Though his theological reading of the entire collection has not produced many converts in the academic community, Eggebrecht's thesis nevertheless demonstrates our collective desire to ascribe a larger purpose to both the *Art of Fugue* and *Musical Offering*. Borrowing analogies from religion, rhetoric, or the stars, we burrow deep into these atypical collections; inevitably, their context in Bach's world competes against their potential for meaning in ours. And there's absolutely nothing wrong with that: Bach, too, embraced this dialectical process—at once historical in methodology and modern in application—in his reception of seminal works by other composers. The organ versets in Frescobaldi's *Fiori musicali*, to return whence this chapter began, had more value for Bach as creative exemplars of learned counterpoint than as liturgical items for the mass, their ostensible purpose in published form. From the moment he acquired a copy of this volume in 1717, Bach's Lutheran milieu determined the nature of his interaction with it.

The earliest admirers of Bach's *Musical Offering* and *Art of Fugue* treated these musical monuments in similar ways—as sources of musical, intellectual, and tactile stimulation. Unlike more geographically connected circles of musicians and trend-setters in places like Paris, the members of Mizler's Society kept abreast of developments in the field through publications, correspondence, and manuscript copying. Its members were part of the professional class, not aristocrats or courtiers, although they sometimes served musically literate rulers like Frederick the Great. Eventually such societies sprang up elsewhere: the Concentores Society, founded in 1798 in London by Haydn pupil John Wall Calcott, fostered the ambitions of composers who made their names writing glees and catches. Bound together by a common pursuit, these groups—of nerds, we might say—kept certain musical traditions alive by sharing within their ranks excellent models for study and inspiration. As Frescobaldi put it in his *Fiori musicali*, in an inscription accompanying a subtly learned dance piece: "Anyone who plays this Bergamasca will learn a lot" (*Chi questa Bergamasca sonara non pocho imparera*). The same may certainly be said about either *Musical Offering* or the *Art of Fugue*.

## SUGGESTIONS FOR FURTHER READING

Those who enjoy tinkering with canon may want to consult journal articles (indexed in this volume's bibliography) by Denis Collins (2001, 2007), Thomas Op de Coul (2006), and Timothy Edwards (2010), all of which address the realization of various canons in *Musical Offering*. Extended allegorical readings of both collections may be found in two books by Hans-Eberhard Dentler: *Johann Sebastian Bachs "Kunst der Fuge": Ein pythagoreisches Werk und seine Verwirklichung* (2004) and *Johann Sebastian Bachs "Musicalisches Opfer": Musik als Abbild der Sphärenharmonie* (2008). For a more explicitly Christian interpretation of the latter work, see Michael Marrisen, "The Theological Character of J. S. Bach's *Musical Offering*" (1995). In *Bach and the Meanings of Counterpoint* (2002), David Yearsley explores the composer's compulsive sense of play with musical styles and procedures as well as societal norms: see especially "The Autocratic Regimes of *A Musical Offering*" (Chapter 4) and "Bach the Machine" (Chapter 5). Peter Williams, finally, in "Frescobaldi's *Fiori musicali* and Bach" (2012), notes numerous parallels between this influential source and several of Bach's late works.

# 5

# Paying Tribute

Though celebrated chiefly as highpoints of the contrapuntal tradition, the *Art of Fugue* and *Musical Offering* also reflect their creator's broad engagement with diverse musical styles, old and new. In this respect Bach was hardly unique; leading composers had long mixed the classic with the fashionable, and by the early eighteenth century this kind of creative assimilation was standard practice among musicians across Europe. Stylistic fusion, as we have seen, can be found throughout the two works that concern us here: the burbly initial subject of Contrapunctus 9 quickly finds a staid partner in the form of the augmented main theme of the *Art of Fugue* (see Example 3.10). Bach reconciled other thematic or topical juxtapositions less felicitously or not at all: the *Ricercar a 3* from *Musical Offering* (on which, see Chapter 3) is a hodgepodge of musical ideas, thanks in part to its origins in improvisation. At the granular level, multiple movements in both collections incorporate up-to-date gestures that punch above their weight in stylistic decorum and allusive import. Such things have ramifications for performance and understanding, as we grapple with Bach's idiosyncratic take on the "mixed style" of composition.

At this point in his career, Bach could afford to treat these projects as experimental and open-ended. Notwithstanding the four-movement sonata in *Musical Offering*, neither follows an established format for a musical edition. Instead, Bach researched systematically his subject matter's contrapuntal potential while devising groups of linked yet contrasting pieces: two ricercari demonstrating free counterpoint *a 3* and strict procedures *a 6*, respectively, and two mirror fugues embracing the stile antico and its

*Bach's* Art of Fugue *and* Musical Offering. Matthew Dirst, Oxford University Press.
© Oxford University Press 2024. DOI: 10.1093/oso/9780197536636.003.0006

stylistic opposite, a lively gigue. He also paid homage in these late learned corpora to prevailing national idioms, with an Italianate *sonata da chiesa* in one and a fugue "in Stylo francese" in the other, and to the voguish galant domain with characteristic gestures in multiple movements of both.

Such allusions or tributes add more than just surface charm; they customize the underlying counterpoint. Bach's contemporaneous arrangements of works by other composers evince a comparable motivation: to honor the legacy of venerable predecessors and prominent contemporaries while modifying their efforts to new ends (whether by adding a continuo line and voice-doubling brass parts to a Palestrina mass or by enriching the texture of Pergolesi's *Stabat Mater* with a more active viola line). Later generations, in turn, paid tribute to the *Art of Fugue* and *Musical Offering* with adaptations and new works of various kinds, in diverse media and disciplines. Assessing these responses to Bach as part of the same historical continuum as his own assimilation of stylistic conventions, I reconsider in this chapter the implications of a few touchstone movements in both collections and reflect on significant moments in their reception.

## Style as Compositional Dress

When we talk about the style of a piece of music, we generally mean the cumulative effect of various compositional strata, which may include the genre or kind of piece, important melodic or rhythmic motives, and a wealth of elaborative detail. The outermost layer of the stylistic onion gives Baroque music its characteristic flavor through a variety of means: obligatory or improvised embellishment, articulation or dynamic inflection of gestures and phrases, and conventional adjustments that performers make to notated rhythmic patterns. Such "seasoning" is essential even in rigorous works like the *Art of Fugue* and *Musical Offering*, both of which include movements that employ the sharply etched rhythmic style often associated with French Baroque music.

In Bach's day the most direct musical route to Paris was the French overture or *ouverture*, an introductory work in two sections whose regal homophonic opening, with its ever-present dotted notes paired with quick upbeat figures, leads to a second section that is generally faster and imitative in nature. (Such pieces had long served to announce the arrival of royalty in the theater, thus lending pomp and ceremony to the beginning of an opera or a ballet. Baroque dance suites often begin with an *ouverture* as well.) Over the course of a long career at church and court, Bach composed numerous *ouvertures* for keyboard solo and for various kinds of ensembles. Although sources of his music may not identify all such pieces as *ouvertures*, neither do all French sources: an *entrée* summons the same mood but in a single section that accompanies the arrival of a central character or a troupe of dancers on the stage. Despite the variety in nomenclature, these movements share a common function: to introduce a larger work or to mark a significant moment in the whole.

Like many of his contemporaries, Bach occasionally employed the characteristic dotted rhythms of the French overture in works associated with royalty of one kind or another. Examples include the *Trauer-Ode* written for the funeral of Queen Christina Eberhardine of Saxony (BWV 198) and the church cantata *Nun komm, der Heiden Heiland* (BWV 61), which entreats the annual liturgical arrival of the Christian Prince of Peace. (The first movement of the former embeds the first four lines of Johann Christoph Gottsched's mourning ode within a churning orchestral ritornello laced with dotted figures and appoggiaturas that summon the majestic and the tragic, respectively. For the opening movement of Cantata 61, Bach embraced both the rhythmic signature and the two-part formal scheme of the *ouverture*, into which he plugged the familiar Advent chorale melody's four phrases, each set in its own distinctive manner.)

In comparable movements without such obvious thematic prompts, Bach sometimes embraced the French style wholeheartedly and at other times just took inspiration from it. For most commentators on *Musical Offering*, a French sensibility sets the interpretive agenda for the *Canon perpetuus super thema regium* (which follows the initial *Ricercar a 3* in the original edition) and the *Canon per Augmentationem, contrario Motu* (the fourth of five *Canones diversi*): Hans T. David (1945), for example, describes the former as an *entrée*. But with just seven measures of three-part counterpoint in realization plus optional repeats, this piece is more royal trifle than tribute, hardly substantial enough for a grand entrance despite its position in the initial engraving as the first of ten canons. That said, its pervasive dotted rhythms and artful extension of the royal theme lend at least a *soupçon* of Frenchness.

Dotted rhythms also figure prominently in the Augmentation Canon, whose accompanying inscription stresses the munificence of one of its primary devices: "As the notes increase, so may the fortunes of the King." While acknowledging the traditional reading of this canon, Marissen (1995) also argues that the longer notes in the augmented voice "deregalize" the whole. Without the quick snap of the original dotted rhythms, this slower-moving voice does indeed lose much of its allegorical connection with the French style; Bach's inscription, in this reading, becomes an ironic jab at Frederick, a humbling reminder of the theology of the cross. But the slower rhythms of the augmented voice contrast audibly with quicker dotted figures in the other two parts, producing an overall texture in which each voice carves out its own identity—not an uncommon occurrence with Bach especially. Perhaps the composer's intention was merely to supply a bit of royal flattery in the usual musical mode for such things, with dotted rhythms of varying lengths.

Detecting sly humor in this piece instead, a Bach-loving scientist once dubbed it the "Sloth Canon." Hofstadter's (1979) comparison, to one of Mother Nature's strangest mammals, makes hay of its juxtaposition of augmentation with melodic inversion, which together mimics the lifestyle of the slow-moving sloth, which hangs from trees upside down. The overall effect of this oddly pokey bit of strict counterpoint may also be summarized with an architectural analogy of my own invention: in contrast with the preceding three canons, whose individual voices convey more ease of movement, the Augmentation Canon is a shuttered musical cloister, whose un-relieved close voicing and grimly formal rhythmic gestures yield a noble yet compact contrapuntal edifice without egress. One may regard this piece, in other words, as simply a demonstration of the royal theme's capacity for artifice, or—more imaginatively—as an allegory on Frederick's fate, as a sendup of his notoriously regi-mented court, or as a comment on the insular nature of counter-point itself. Take your pick.

For performers, the pervasive dotted rhythms of such pieces oblige at least some familiarity with Baroque performance conventions. From the first appearance of the *ouverture* in the stage music of Jean-Baptiste Lully, the notation of its rhythms was often approximate, rendering negotiable the length of notes in dotted figures, with much depending on the player's sense of style. Musicians of this era, regardless of nationality, knew to interpret notation with a grain of salt; contemporaneous writers on music describe, in multiple sources, how to lengthen dotted notes and shorten upbeat figures in the performance of *ouvertures* and other French-style pieces. Though it fell into disuse after 1800 or so, "overdotting" (as we now call it) reemerged in the mid twentieth century for performance of this repertoire. But because contem-porary understanding of this custom, even among professionals, tends to rely on normative practice more than nuanced distinctions between works, it will be instructive to consider its application in a more substantial French-style piece: Contrapunctus 6, subtitled in the original print of the *Art of Fugue* "in Stylo francese" ("in the French style").

Bach's autograph manuscript puts this fugue seventh in the overall order, a position it shares with a potential model from a col-lection that may have provided inspiration for the whole. George

Stauffer (1983) first noticed that Mattheson's *Die wohlklingende Fingersprache* and Bach's hand copy of the *Art of Fugue* follow a similar order of fugal manners or types. Stauffer's hunch may be extended to matters of style as well: just as the sixth fugue in each is premised on two subjects, their respective seventh fugues feature dotted rhythms. Like much French-style music of this era, both fugues mix slow and fast dotted rhythms throughout, as Example 5.1 shows. While their respective notation may be realized precisely, some performers opt to sharpen the slower gestures so that single eighth notes fall together with single sixteenths. In the case of Contrapunctus 6, that kind of adjustment has profound consequences: one trades contrapuntal independence for a consistent rhythmic style.

**Example 5.1** (a) Johann Mattheson, *Die wohlklingende Fingersprache*, Fugue VII, mm. 6–9; (b) *Contrapunctus 6*, mm. 1–4

In his 1952 study of the *Art of Fugue*, the pioneering Dutch harpsichordist Gustav Leonhardt argued for precisely this kind of adjustment, with lengthened dotted quarters and shortened eighth notes throughout Contrapunctus 6. Because he also added dots to all evenly notated groups of sixteenth notes in this fugue, Leonhardt felt obliged to provide a partial transcription in an appendix, to aid players who might realize its rhythms as notated and thereby "destroy much of [its] musical value . . . giving it a somewhat limping character." Other prominent harpsichordists embrace at least the former modification without question: Davitt Moroney recommends it in his popular edition of the work and David Schulenberg, in his comprehensive study of the Bach keyboard works, finds it "hard to object" to overdotted quarter notes in this piece. And yet, leaving the rhythms as Bach left them in the original print poses little danger of rhythmic impairment; on the contrary, this kind of approach avoids a few otherwise anomalous moments. Lengthening the dotted quarters throughout Contrapunctus 6 requires, notably, a change to the opening subject entry, which has no partner voice with which to coordinate its initial dotted figure. There is, in other words, no musical reason (beyond the subtitle) to lengthen the first dot.

One might also argue more generally against such adjustments in fugue: the signature rhythm of a French overture typically animates only its initial (primarily chordal) section, not the imitative section that follows. When Bach wanted dotted figures to be sharpened in performance, he took pains to be explicit with notation, as the multiple surviving versions of the Overture in the French Manner (BWV 831) demonstrate. By contrast, both the Augmentation Canon and Contrapunctus 6 are imitative pieces whose surface rhythms pay homage to the French style (like the Fugue in D major from *WTC 1* or the fughetta on *Wir glauben all' an einen Gott* from *Clavier-Übung III*), not French overtures in need of overdotting. The subtitle of Contrapunctus 6 is perhaps best understood as an acknowledgement of the stylistic orientation of this fugue, not a rhythmic directive for players. Given Bach's repeated use of the dotted variant of the main theme, which serves as the melodic engine for all three counter-fugues (Contrapuncti 5, 6, and 7), performers may prefer to accept the minor voice leading infelicities that simultaneous eighth- and sixteenth-note pickups eventually produce in Contrapunctus 6. Only twice in this piece (in mm. 65 and 76) does Bach oblige a choice between two note values on the same pitch at the same time, forcing keyboardists to play one or the other while leaving chamber musicians free to realize the notes without adjustment.

An additional argument against overdotting in Contrapunctus 6 may be adduced from the Augmentation Canon in *Musical Offering*. Sharpening the dotted rhythms of this similarly Frenchified canon would undercut Bach's inscription, which depends entirely on enlarged values for all notes of the derived voice. A blanket adjustment of notated rhythms in Contrapunctus 6 would likewise obscure its juxtaposition of multiple variants of the fugue subject. Ultimately, such a change privileges a convention of performance—one crucial, in this case, only in another genre—over more fundamental aspects of composition.

Whether one plays the notes as printed or not, this fugue's overt allusion to the French style, as Dreyfus (1996) observes, is inevitably subsumed by its relentless drive and linear complexity, which make it one of the most challenging in the volume to execute. Complex stylistic mixtures like these became more common over the course of Bach's lifetime, as an expanding market for keyboard and chamber music encouraged novelty in the 1730s and 1740s especially. Experimentation came with attendant risks, however: immoderate assimilation of disparate stylistic elements prompted the occasional broadside from critics who lamented transparent efforts to amplify expression from composers who lacked the necessary imagination and technical finesse. More critical salvo than censure, such opinions nevertheless built consensus among writers on music for a new stylistic decorum, one that put a premium on clarity as opposed to the more layered approach to composition typical of the generation of Bach and Handel.

Because Bach pushed the envelope aggressively in this regard, he became a primary target for progressive critics like Johann Adolph Scheibe, who decried the "turgid and confused" nature of the Leipzig cantor's church music while extolling his Italian Concerto (BWV 971) as a "perfect model of a well-designed solo concerto . . . a piece that deserves emulation by

**Example 5.2**  Prelude in A♭ Major from *WTC 1*, mm. 1–4

all our great composers." Scheibe's fondness for the latter surely extended to simpler pieces in which one might find, say, an elementary bit of keyboard figuration casually tossed between the hands (Example 5.2). Bach's clever melding of disparate idioms occasionally subverts expectations even in heavily procedural movements: a fugue might adopt the swinging rhythms of a gigue, thereby cloaking learnedness in modish dress (Example 5.3). In comparison, his stretto-laden Contrapunctus 6 seems designed to confound most contemporaries. Even modern writers on music, with the benefit of considerable research into Bach's compositional practice, have often wondered what to make of his most thoroughgoing stylistic mixtures, from this French-style fugue to overtly galant movements in *Musical Offering*.

**Example 5.3**  Fugue in G Major from *WTC 1*, mm. 1–4

The latter term, as bandied about by the urban *beau monde* of Bach's day, encompassed elegant manners and customs, pleasant pastimes, visual art or literature on pastoral themes, and tuneful or *cantabile* music that relies principally on easygoing, singing melodies in short, repeated phrases above a predictable and often static accompaniment. Despite its French origins, German writers on music had more to say about the genteel galant than did their French counterparts, whose publications barely mention it. For Scheibe the word implied transparency and even eloquence, without excessive erudition. In all its varied manifestations, the intellectual wherewithal to participate in cultivated society without breaking a sweat was assumed: galant was the eighteenth-century equivalent of "cool."

Even before he ascended the throne, Frederick the Great embodied the ideal of the *galant homme*, meaning an individual with a keen intellect and an unerring sense of style. Through sheer force of will, and despite a despotic and philistinic father, Frederick read widely and surrounded himself with leading scientists, philosophers, artists, and musicians. With strong opinions about virtually every aspect of culture, he transformed Berlin from a backwater into a vibrant capital city while imposing on it his own agenda. This presented Sebastian Bach with a unique if daunting opportunity in 1747: to impress an enlightened monarch while flattering his keen musical sensibilities. Obliging Frederick's request for fugues on a thoroughly recondite theme, Bach also created a substantial centerpiece in his *Musical Offering*: a four-movement sonata scored smartly for an ensemble that includes the flute, the royal instrument. Having produced relatively little chamber music for the standard combination of two melody instruments plus continuo, Bach embraced it wholeheartedly in this ambitious sonata, which mingles the sober royal theme with the hyper-expressive Berlin galant.

Bach was no newcomer to this game, having threaded many a stylistic needle in a variety of genres and media. The title page of his keyboard partitas offers a useful reminder, with its description of the volume's contents as "preludes, allemandes, courantes . . . and other galanteries composed for music lovers, to refresh their spirits." Whether for talented students like Johann Ludwig Krebs or for a gifted amateur like Luise Gottsched, wife of the Leipzig philosopher and poet, such language hit all the right notes for these dance suites, which are also infused with a strongly contrapuntal ethos. Capitalizing on the genre's popularity and perhaps in response to Handel's celebrated *Suites de Pièces pour le Clavecin* (1720), Bach had each partita engraved separately between 1726 and 1730 before republishing them in 1731 in a single large volume as *Clavier-Übung I*; an additional work in this idiom, the luxurious *Ouvertüre nach Französischer Art*, appeared in *Clavier-Übung II* in 1735. Simpler dance and character pieces by other composers, in the meantime, became the favored repertoire of bourgeois keyboard players, who were kept supplied by printing houses that fed growing demand with increasing numbers of editions toward mid-century.

In the occasional concerted work from this time, Bach subjected familiar conventions of the galant to more extended critique. The protagonists of his 1729 secular cantata *The Dispute between Phoebus & Pan* (BWV 201), for instance, engage in a singing contest borrowed from Greek mythology, which Picander's shrewd libretto reframes as an argument about style. Phoebus gives voice to the high style with flowery verses about the handsome youth Hyacinth, while Pan embraces the low style with lyrics redolent of a court buffoon. An additional layer of humor comes from Bach's musical setting, which borrows features of the galant for both title characters' arias. Phoebus, who sings first, is surrounded by a lush ensemble of strings and winds whose multiple embellished obbligatos add layers of fancy window dressing above his suggestive text, with its intimation of forbidden love. But his aria's predictable phrase structure and underlying rhythm are that of a simple minuet: it's a *galanterie* in full drag. Out of Pan's mouth, in the rejoinder aria, comes a hilarious stutter on "wack-ack-ack-ack-ack-ack-ackelt das Herz" ("my heart sha-a-a-a-a-akes"). Those alert to Pan's musical surroundings, which comprise a buoyant obbligato for unison violins plus an equally perky continuo line, may discover that his aria's leading idea is endlessly imitative, unlike the swoony arabesques of Phoebus's ostensibly more artful song. Such subtle play with musical signifiers can be found even in monumental sacred works like the Mass in B Minor, where they generally carry less subversive messages: the lilting melody of "Domine Deus" or the repetitive melodic gestures of "Et in Spiritum sanctum," for example.

With more abstract ends in mind in his late instrumental cycles, Bach put counterpoint itself into a complex dialectic with the galant. His willingness to experiment engendered, among other things, a sonata that raised considerable interest after its 1747 publication, to judge from the number of surviving hand copies from the late eighteenth century of just this printing unit from the original edition of *Musical Offering*. Despite its singular intensity, the sonata remains the most popular item in the collection. Its formidable reputation among players began early: in 1781, Bach's student Johann Philipp Kirnberger, music master to Frederick's sister Anna Amalia, published a partial realization of its continuo part in his treatise on figured bass as a demonstration piece for readers, few of whom could possibly have contemplated such a gnarly bass line in their own chamber playing. Subsequent writers have wondered openly whether Bach simply went too far with this piece. Hans Vogt (1981/88), for one, frets that the sonata "might be too rambling, too tiring . . . [because] Bach had reached a stage of maturity at which he no longer concerned himself much with questions of interpretation and reception." Others have sought to explain its eccentricities as barely concealed efforts to lampoon the Berlin court's attachment to the galant style. Its "elegantly melancholy passages," writes James Gaines (2005), "are just this side of cheap . . . guaranteed to make audiences swoon."

Apologists typically point to its Andante, whose beginning appears as Example 5.4, as the most problematic movement. Notably absent here is the royal theme, which emerges obliquely in the opening Largo's pulsing bassline and with greater clarity in both fast movements. The Andante begins instead with a slowly rising motive in the flute and violin above a gently oscillating tonic pedal. This leisurely intonation leads to a pair of faster *amphibrach* motives in the melody instruments (the related poetic foot comprises three syllables: unstressed-stressed-unstressed), a process Bach repeats (in m. 2) to complete the harmonic period. Treble and bass ideas exchange registers after the downbeat of the

**Example 5.4** Sonata from *Musical Offering*, Andante (iii), mm. 1–7

third bar, as in the Prelude in A♭ major cited above, but a sleight of hand in the continuo part (mm. 3–4) manipulates the initial rising and falling motive to modulate upward. The ensuing chromatic descent in the continuo accompanies an increasingly insistent series of amphibrachs above, to which Bach adds (in m. 6) a carefully staggered pair of melodic cascades. This intricate mix of motives glides gently (m. 7) into the movement's first cadence.

Bach's contemporaries may well have wondered: is this a tribute to or a caricature of the galant? Or is it both? Few pieces in the repertoire mix gravity and insouciance so thoroughly. The amphibrach dominates the Andante to an extraordinary degree, with recurrences in every bar (often several times) and on every beat of mm. 24–27. Frequent shifts between *forte* and *piano* in the flute and violin parts, coupled with modulations to B♭ minor and A♭ major (evil keys for all involved), add drama and a dash of uncertainty throughout. Using just the opening bars as a prompt, a less driven composer might have produced a thoroughly conventional *affettuoso* or *espressivo*-style movement with a consistent phraseology and straightforward harmonic plan. Bach's systematic exploration of his motivic material generated something more unusual: a galant yet *recherché* species of three-part counterpoint whose frequent swoops and sighs verge on the irrational. Closer to the general aesthetic of this era, which valued balanced expression, is the Prelude in F Minor from *WTC 2*, whose similar gestures (delivered in parallel thirds and sixths, as in the Andante) rotate in and out of the texture politely. The Andante from *Musical Offering*, with its quicksilver emotional content, conjures instead the *Empfindsamer stil* or "sentimental style" of the Berlin court ensemble—perhaps too well.

## Adaptation and Homage

Like most of his peers, Bach recycled his own music occasionally, fitting new texts to vocal works or rescoring sonatas or concertos for new combinations of instruments as needed. His two-keyboard arrangement of Contrapunctus 13 from the *Art of Fugue* made an otherwise formidable pair of pieces (*rectus* and *inversus*) more approachable for highly skilled players like Anna Amalia, who may have played her copy with the assistance of either Kirnberger or Agricola, the Bach pupils in her circle. Sebastian Bach likely suggested another transcription relevant to our present concerns: a fragment (*c*1747–48) of the opening movement of the sonata from *Musical Offering*, in the hand of his youngest son J. C. F. Bach, rescores this Largo for obbligato harpsichord and either flute or violin. Extant hand copies from mid-century also include C. P. E.

Bach's arrangement of the *Fuga canonica* from the same collection for violin and obbligato harpsichord (probably for a private concert at his home) and a similarly scored copy by J. C. Oley that designates either violin or flute for the upper voice.

Arrangements from subsequent decades show patterns emerging early in the reception of individual movements. Agricola was among the first to transcribe the *Ricercar a 6* for organ, while a c1800 Viennese transcription of the same fugue for strings expands the list of potential participants to at least nine, with doublet parts for the top three lines and single parts for the rest. Contrapunctus 8 also found enthusiastic chamber players: W. A. Mozart arranged it for string trio (KV 404a), and around 1800 an unidentified hand transcribed it for two keyboards.

The Bach publishing industry, which got started in the years around 1800 with multiple volumes of the keyboard and various chamber works, eventually turned to "interpretive" editions that expanded the spirit of contemporaneous transcriptions with more explicit performance directives. Among the most notorious of these is an 1838 volume comprising the *Art of Fugue* and both ricercari from *Musical Offering*, as prepared by pianist and pedagogue Carl Czerny for Breitkopf & Härtel in Leipzig. Czerny's dynamic and articulation marks, added ostensibly to reflect Beethoven's manner of playing Bach, caused a scandal for the publisher, with prominent figures like Schumann and Mendelssohn decrying such editorial intervention with Bach's music. Breitkopf issued a revision barely a year later under a different editor, and at least two reissues followed. (The 1841 impression, supervised by an unnamed "committee of artists," offered the first detailed analysis of the work from music theorist Moritz Hauptmann, who would soon become Bach's successor as Cantor of the St. Thomas School.) Though controversial, Czerny's foregrounding of thematic material in Bach fugues made good sense of the change in equipment over time: the piano encourages dynamic shading, something harpsichordists can only approximate through articulation, voicing, and timing. As

I have argued elsewhere (Dirst 2012), one can see in earlier string transcriptions of Bach fugues the seeds of this familiar habit: in parts prepared by Mozart, consistent articulation marks highlight all subject entries, encouraging a uniform delivery of the theme throughout, irrespective of the occasional concealed or elided entry. These sources and others like it suggest that just thirty years or so after Bach's death, the way musicians thought about and experienced fugue had changed profoundly, with imitative textures obliging players to favor thematic over non-thematic material.

The subject of the "Prussian Fugue," a nickname that Bach himself used for the entire *Musical Offering*, resonated strongly among composers of Mozart's generation, inspiring several new works that betray minimal interest in Bach's distinctive musical language. Unlike more extensive homages from later eras, the earliest works in this vein rehearse just the first five notes of the royal theme without subjecting it to extended interrogation. Giovanni Paisiello's *Les Adieux de la Grande Duchesse de Russies* (c1783), for example, begins with Frederick's opening triad and diminished seventh (transposed to D minor) but otherwise steers clear of counterpoint. (Composed during Paisiello's years at the court of Catherine the Great in Saint Petersburg, this energetic capriccio for piano with violin was later abridged and arranged by an unknown hand for piano solo.) Friedrich Wilhelm Rust, grandfather of the nineteenth-century Thomaskantor and Bach scholar Wilhelm Rust, used the same five notes as the first theme of the opening and closing movements of his Sonata in D minor for violin and piano (c1788). (F. W. Rust had multiple connections to the Bach tradition, including a brother who played violin for Sebastian Bach in Leipzig. Though the former Rust spent most of his life in Dessau, he went to Berlin in 1764 for composition study with Franz Benda; while there, he likely interacted with both W. F. and C. P. E. Bach. More than twenty years later, he composed this *Sonata per Cembalo o Forte piano con Violino*, as the manuscript has it, though no trace of its violin part survives. Vincent d'Indy made some adjustments

to its closing movement for his 1913 edition of twelve Rust key-.
board sonatas, where it appears as No. 7.)

Entire themes from *Musical Offering* and the *Art of Fugue* eventually found their way into new music by composers with a stronger
affinity for Bachian counterpoint. Johannes Brahms's Sonata No.
1 for cello and piano, Op. 38 (1862–65), exemplifies this mode of
engagement. For the subject of its fugal finale, Brahms borrowed
from the theme of Contrapunctus 13 a few tell-tale features: an initial octave leap plus chains of busy triplets and some strategically
placed long notes (Example 5.5). Like Bach, Brahms made the most
of his theme's contrapuntal potential but within a vigorous sonata-
allegro movement that incorporates, after its initial exposition,
sophisticated devices like inversion and stretto. The same sonata's
opening movement, enriched with a comparable dose of invertible
counterpoint, begins with a theme whose general contours recall
the subject of Contrapunctus 3. More pervasive borrowing from
the *Art of Fugue* provides essential structure for Ferruccio Busoni's
bombastic *Fantasia contrappuntistica* (1910), which incorporates
the final unfinished fugue plus other bits and pieces from Bach's
collection, all plumped up as if on steroids.

**Example 5.5** (a) Contrapunctus 13 *inversus*, mm. 1–3; (b) Brahms,
Sonata No. 1 for Cello and Piano, Op 38, Allegro (iii), mm. 1–3

Against this historical backdrop, a revolutionary kind of Bach
transcription emerged from the Second Viennese School. These
adaptations effectively transformed their originals by means of

*Klangfarbenmelodie*, in which several instruments or families of instruments play conjoined segments of individual musical lines. One of the best-known examples of "tone-color melody," as pioneered by Arnold Schoenberg, is a 1935 transcription of Bach's *Ricercar a 6* by Anton Webern. Significant experience as a conductor of contemporary music also informs the latter's *Fuga (Ricercata) a 6 voci*, which, as Webern himself declared, liberates Bach's celebrated six-part fugue from the confines of keyboard performance. Notably, Webern added not a single note to this piece; even the quiet timpani rolls that occasionally precede entrances of the royal theme are rooted in Bach's own pedal points. Instead, this technicolor transcription "awakens what is still sleeping" in the work by highlighting individual motives within its contrapuntal fabric. In shape-shifting lines that interpret this fugue anew, as the musically minded philosopher Theodor Adorno put it, Webern's elegantly dovetailed instruments declaim Bach's dense and discursive texture with disarming rhetoric.

Characterizing this epochal arrangement as a "clarification of the contrapuntal structure" of the original, musicologist Carl Dahlhaus (1987) agreed with Schoenberg on the fundamental necessity of such intervention in the modern age, since we routinely prioritize motivic over contrapuntal procedures in our music-making. (Those who value both may choose to listen to Webern's homage with Bach's score in hand, thereby keeping the eye and mind informed while the ear enjoys multi-hued counterpoint.) Subsequent transcriptions brought renewed attention to the entirety of Bach's *Musical Offering*. A 1950 orchestration by the Ukrainian composer and conductor Igor Markevitch, to mention only one of many later transcriptions, sets the individual voices of both ricercari with more consistency though with less imagination than Webern; Markevitch's realizations of some of the canons, on the other hand, are ingenious.

In 1980 Webern's *Fuga* begat a more innovative descendent in an *Offertorium* for solo violin and orchestra by Tartar-Russian composer Sofia Gubaidulina. Composed for violinist Gidon

Kremer, who subsequently championed and recorded it, this remarkable work pays simultaneous tribute to Bach and Webern. Gubaidulina, too, cloaks the royal theme in *Klangfarbenmelodie*, but there the similarity with Webern ends; she uses Frederick's melody as a recurring portal for a series of increasingly deconstructed variations that assume different characters from one moment to the next. Her score shuttles seamlessly between traditional and graphic notational styles, whose mixing in the solo violin and orchestral parts produce passages of ethereal color, momentary violence, and tender longing. The ending is particularly evocative: what sounds like a harmonized ecclesiastical chant coalesces slowly, in somber and hushed tones accompanied by a gradual reconstruction, in whiffs and snatches, of the royal theme in retrograde.

Seven years before Webern published his transcription of the *Ricercar a 6*, an orchestration of the *Art of Fugue* introduced this work in its entirety to the concertgoing public at a performance in the Leipzig Thomaskirche, under cantor Karl Straube's direction as part of the 1927 Bach Festival. Swiss *wunderkind* Wolfgang Graeser (1906–1928) made the arrangement, one of several transcriptions of the work now attributed to him. This luxuriously scored *Art of Fugue* (for string quartet plus a full complement of strings, winds, harpsichord, and organ) found its champions and dozens of performances followed. Its popularity waned within a decade or so, however. Some prominent figures faulted its basic premise (as Heinrich Husmann argued in a 1938 essay pointedly entitled "Die Kunst der Fuge als Klavierwerk") while others denounced Graeser as the instigator of a veritable flood of *Art of Fugue* arrangements, with one prickly author dismissing the lot as "emollients for the jaded or unimaginative." Although Graeser's novel order for the *Art of Fugue* has also fallen by the wayside, his meticulous comparison of an old edition of the work (likely that of the Swiss publisher Nägeli) against the autograph produced significant and lasting results: in 1924 the *Bach-Jahrbuch* published a detailed essay by the budding eighteen-year-old scholar, and in 1926 Breitkopf & Härtel followed suit with a reprinting of the *Art of Fugue* in a revised edition by Graeser. (The latter was released as a Supplement to the Bach Gesellschaft, whose 1878 edition of the work by Wilhelm Rust differs in significant respects.)

Scholarship on the *Art of Fugue* was not sufficient, however, for an advocate like Graeser, who wanted the German *Volk* to reflect on this "valuable treasure of our nation . . . fallen into shameful forgetfulness," hence his efforts to enable performances of it. As Michael Markham (2001) has pointed out, these words echo Spitta's (1880) complaint that this work "never yet formed part of the life of the German nation," despite its "incomparable perfection and depth of feeling." Spitta's emotional response to Bach's learned corpus failed to rouse most of his academic colleagues, who chose to ignore the messy business of interpretation for the *Art of Fugue* especially. This scholarly predisposition, still common in theoretical analyses, has affected writing about this work more than perhaps any other of Bach, rendering it somehow immune to sentiment or passion though open to metaphorical description or allegorical interpretation. Even Albert Schweitzer, who tutored French organist Charles-Marie Widor on the colorful rhetoric of Bach's chorale preludes, described in his 1908 Bach monograph the main theme of the *Art of Fugue* as a gateway into "a still and serious world, deserted and rigid, without color, without light, without motion."

Reception among the Germans especially gravitated toward a metaphysical conception of Bach's most learned works: Graeser considered the *Art of Fugue* "pure abstraction." At that point, "earthly realization" of its contents could be "left to others," as Richard Benz observed in a 1935 book entitled *Bachs Geistiges Reich* (*Bach's Spiritual Empire*). Central for German writers of this era, who situated Bach squarely at the head of their own dominant musical tradition, was the conviction that this work "captures in its unfolding the essence of the will to power," as Markham writes.

Leaving aside the appropriation of such ideas by contemporary political figures, we might consider how this strand of reception engaged with the larger cultural sphere of its day. Graeser himself provided a handy bridge to other disciplines in his "Schematic Plan" for the *Art of Fugue,* published in an Appendix to the Bach Gesellschaft Supplement. This truss-like graphic (Figure 5.1) summarizes what was, for this generation, one of the work's central attractions: structural logic as reflected in multiple internal symmetries. Such things, as it happened, fascinated more than just early twentieth-century Bach scholars. For creative types of all kinds, the greatness of an artwork had come to rely, first and foremost, on its formal strength.

Of particular interest to the musically inclined artists of the Blaue Reiter circle in Munich and especially of the Bauhaus (1919–33), the Weimar Republic's iconic laboratory for art and design, were the interlocking patterns of counterpoint and fugue as exemplified in Bach's music. This first wave of "expressionist" artists (as we now call them) produced, in didactic writings and in creative work, new ways of visualizing the interplay between the temporal and the geometric, thanks in part to Bach. Paul Klee, perhaps the most pedagogically inclined of his cohort, believed that an understanding of polyphony could improve the experience of visual art for the beholder, who would then be better prepared "to penetrate deep into the cosmic sphere," to borrow language from *The Thinking Eye* (1961), a collection of the artist's 1921–22 Bauhaus lectures. "The simultaneity of several independent themes," Klee affirmed, "is something that is possible not only in music" but can in fact be found "everywhere and anywhere."

Illustrating his ideas with an actual piece, Klee emphasized the functional distinctions between three obbligato lines in the Adagio from Bach's Sonata in G Major for violin and harpsichord (BWV 1019/4). This intricate yet flexible module of three-part counterpoint had obvious resonance for Klee's students, for whom he created a graph of the entire movement, which he considered "abstract and at the same time compellingly real."

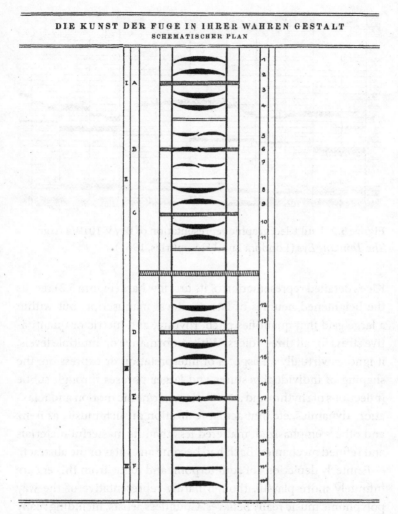

**Figure 5.1** "Schematic Plan" for the *Art of Fugue* by Wolfgang Graeser, from the Bach Gesellschaft Supplement to the work (1926)

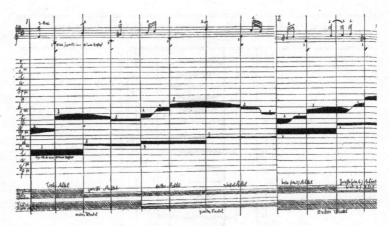

**Figure 5.2**  Paul Klee, graphic representation of BWV 1019/4 from *The Thinking Eye* (London: Lund Humphries, 1961).

Klee's detailed representation of its first few bars (Figure 5.2) recalls the heightened neumes of late-medieval manuscripts but within a large grid that quantifies pitch, rhythm, and metric or quantitative stress for all three voices. While informative on multiple levels, it ignores virtually all aspects of interpretation or expression: the shaping of individual gestures and larger phrases through subtle inflections of rhythm and articulation, harmonic motion and relaxation, dynamics, etc. But actual realization of such music, as Benz and others emphasized, mattered less than its masterful materials and refined mechanics. Bach had become an avatar of the abstract.

Painterly depictions of counterpoint and fugue from this era are infinitely more playful, though hardly representative of the way polyphonic music really behaves. Countless artists, including many of the first rank, reimagined fugue visually during the 1910s and 20s, as Peter Vergo (2010) has documented. Some used repeating shapes arrayed linearly to convey the way musical ideas might be repeated, transposed, overlapped, and otherwise manipulated: Klee's kinetic *Fugue in Red* (1921) and Joseph Albers' grid-like *Fugue* (1926) are perhaps the best-known examples of this species of allusion. Georges Braque's *Homage à J. S. Bach* (1911–12) offers instead a thoroughly saturated Cubist jumble of geometric shapes, but its underlying organization reflects, as Vergo observes, the contemporary understanding of an inscrutable yet orderly Bach, the composer of cerebral counterpoint. For these artists, Bach fugues provided inspiration for their own comparably brainy creations, for which they devised a new approach to representation that mixed mechanical reproduction with transcendental aesthetics.

Alongside this time-honored view of fugue as an exemplification of cosmic order, fugue's capacity to signal disorder has been apparent since at least the early eighteenth century, as Joel Greenberg (2018) reminds us. Bach himself took advantage of this alternative potential in fugal movements for angry mobs: the hard-edged imitation of "Sind Blitze, sind Donner" in the *Matthew Passion* hammers upwards by fourths in this whirlwind chorus, in defiance of the standard alternation of tonic and dominant subject entries. By the early twentieth century, the disruptive side of counterpoint and fugue occasionally reared its head in more than just strictly musical contexts—from the cornucopia of colorful, wiggling shapes in Wassily Kandinsky's eye-popping *Fuga* (1914) to a fictional character hopelessly confused by equally insistent contrapuntal lines in Aldous Huxley's *Point Counter Point* (1928). In the relevant passage of this biting and much-discussed *roman à clef*, Huxley gives voice to an ailing artist by the name of John Bidlake, who tries but fails to make sense of a famous fugue by Bach. The imitative section from the opening movement of the "Orchestral" Suite in B Minor begins promisingly, as Huxley writes, with a "clear, definite, unmistakable" initial subject and subsequent entries of equally "separate and individual" voices; but their eventual combination produces utter chaos. "The resultant noise," Bidlake bitterly concludes, "means something perhaps to the statistician, nothing to the artist."

Taking the bait several decades later, an interdisciplinary scholar reconsidered, within the context of an ambitious study of rule-based systems, what Bach may be trying to tell us in his *Musical Offering* and *Art of Fugue*, among other works. Winner of a Pulitzer Prize, Douglas Hofstadter's thought-provoking *Gödel, Escher, Bach* is an extended philosophical meditation on complex systems of various kinds, including music. A polymath whose primary interest is cognition itself, Hofstadter alternates scientific chapters with fictional interludes that feature goofy characters popularized by Lewis Carroll. Bach's music provides (in the latter) either diversion or structure for the eccentric conversations of Tortoise, Achilles, and Mr. Crab—which, in turn, lampoon shibboleths of mathematics, philosophy, and artificial intelligence while helping the reader to come to grips with complex systems in technology as well as art. Musical puns abound, as do penetrating observations about how we process information and create meaning.

The culminating *divertissement* in this now-classic tome begins as a musical salon at the Crab residence but becomes, through a series of wondrous detours, a *tour-de-force* verbal fugue. Only here in *Gödel, Escher, Bach* does Hofstadter expand his narrative boundaries into metafiction by supplementing his three amigos with a few surprise guests, including the author himself plus two pivotal British mathematicians: Charles Babbage, who with his 1837 Analytical Engine invented the computer, and Alan Turing, whose eponymous machine made computer science possible. Babbage also occasionally conjures the spirit of J. S. Bach, with Crab channeling Frederick the Great—who, in an inspired passage, cheerfully returns the ten canons from *Musical Offering* to their creator. Tying up various loose ends, Hofstadter summons in this final comedy all individual components of his favorite musical source, with spirited conversation that occasionally enacts learned devices. Bach's RICERCAR acrostic plays a prominent role in twelve distinct iterations, which mimic the twelve soundings of the royal theme in the *Ricercar a 6*. Surpassing even Bach, Hofstadter slips in one retrograde statement: "Regarding Artistic Canons, Retrogression's Elusive; Contrariwise, Inversion's Recognizable."

Whizzing and whirring at the center of this tall tale are Crab's latest "smart-stupid" computers, which he invites Babbage to take for a test drive. Artful shenanigans ensue, including a game of chess and a request for a simulated intelligence six times greater than that of His Crabness. Babbage dutifully produces such a virtual being in the form of Turing, who promptly claims to have invented Babbage. At this point, the vignette becomes a bewildering game of wits, with Turing and Babbage trading places inside and outside the screen, thoroughly confusing Crab, Achilles, and Tortoise. The author restores order by pulling back the curtain on his literary ricercar, but not before it has paid tribute to Sebastian Bach by transporting learned contrapuntal games into the world of thinking machines.

At the very end, the assembled characters finally come together for their original objective: an evening of chamber playing of selected movements from *Musical Offering*. A last-minute request from Achilles appends the "Endlessly Rising Canon" to the *Ricercar a 6*, thereby ensuring that at least one of Bach's "strange loops" lingers in the reader's imagination. Hofstadter's larger message, that Bach's favored modes of musical play are comparable to the processes and mechanisms that enable our continually expanding virtual universe, is well taken. I would add only that Bach's music has had greater staying power than even the finest of computer codes.

## SUGGESTIONS FOR FURTHER READING

Much of the scholarly writing on Bach's assimilation of stylistic currents—whether French, Italian, galant, or otherwise—focuses on questions of performance practice or on his adaptation of discrete stylistic conventions. For a more nuanced view that examines this issue within the larger intellectual climate of Bach's day, see Laurence Dreyfus, "Bach as a Critic of Enlightenment" (Chapter 8 in his *Bach and the Patterns of Invention*, 1996). Reception studies, on the other hand, are often organized around the practices of specific communities and individuals or around epochal events like the 1829 revival of the *Matthew Passion*. On crucial developments in early twentieth-century reception of the *Ricercar a 6* and the *Art of Fugue*, see especially Carl Dahlhaus, "Bach's Six-Part Ricercar as Orchestrated by Anton Webern" (1987) and Michael Markham, "'The Usefulness of Such Artworks': Expression, Analysis, and Nationalism in *The Art of Fugue*" (2001). Peter Vergo's *The Music of Painting* (2010), alternatively, features a wide-ranging chapter that addresses Bach's influence on modern art.

# 6

# Elusive Ideals

> While working on this fugue, in which the name BACH
> appears in the countersubject, the composer died.

At some point after his father's death on July 28, 1750, C. P. E. Bach
added this terse statement to the autograph materials for the *Art
of Fugue*, on the very page where a mammoth compound fugue
on three subjects peters out quietly, without a proper conclusion
(Figure 6.1). One suspects that Emanuel penned these words principally for friends with whom he shared this precious document,
which eventually passed into the hands of Georg Johann Daniel
Poelchau before landing in the Berlin state library. Wittingly or
not, C. P. E. Bach endowed this fugue (and by extension, the entire collection) with a certain mystique: J. S. Bach died with pen in
hand while struggling to complete his ultimate fugal compendium.
Despite evidence that the elder Bach ceased work on the *Art of
Fugue* several months earlier, the familiar image of the great contrapuntist on his deathbed endures—thus we contemplate what might
have been.

Notwithstanding the precise chronology of the unfinished
fugue, the lack of more notes will always bother; its unquestioned
authenticity obliges even those who regard it as extraneous to
the larger work to explain its origins and Bach's intentions for it.
Nagging questions about this and other portions of the *Art of Fugue*
and *Musical Offering*, as we have seen, tend to be answered with informed hypotheses rather than firm conclusions. This means that
anyone wrestling with this music faces some peculiar choices, from

*Bach's* Art of Fugue *and* Musical Offering. Matthew Dirst, Oxford University Press.
© Oxford University Press 2024. DOI: 10.1093/oso/9780197536636.003.0007

**Figure 6.1** Final page of the unfinished fugue from Bach's autograph manuscript of the *Art of Fugue* (from m. 227, beat 3)

the proper constitution and order of these works to the conundrum of incompleteness. Focusing on unresolved or otherwise open-ended issues in both collections, I argue in this concluding chapter for a manner of engagement inspired by but not limited to that of Bach's own day.

To begin with the gap: like Contrapuncti 8–11, the unfinished fugue explores sequentially the combinatorial potential of multiple subjects, each of which animates a discrete section that eventually incorporates previously introduced thematic material. A grave initial subject, seemingly distilled from the main theme of the *Art of Fugue* but lacking its pivotal leading tone, generates an expansive opening section full of luxurious sequences and harmonies. An equally long second section features a chipper, more modern subject that becomes an adroit partner to the first theme in various combinations. For his third theme Bach selected four notes that correspond to his own surname, a favorite motive from his musical clan's bag of tricks. (In German musical nomenclature, the letter "B" denotes B♭ and "H" is B♮.) This concise yet stubbornly chromatic fugue subject, which produces some hair-raising modulations, culminates on the page depicted here in a single revealing combination of all three themes deployed simultaneously (from m. 234), after which the individual voices simply disappear, leaving a final dangling bar of inconclusive passagework in the tenor.

Unlike the previous sections, this one lacks definitive closure. As such, the "Fuga a 3 Soggetti" (as the original edition of the *Art of Fugue* calls it) must have shocked more than a few subscribers, for whom an unfinished fugue in a published volume would have made no sense. Acknowledging with apology its incompleteness, Emanuel Bach and Agricola papered over the problem in their edition by suppressing the autograph's final seven bars: the engraved print stops at the preceding Phrygian half cadence on the dominant instead (with the descent from B♭ to A in the bass at the downbeat of m. 233). This effectively concealed—for more than a century—the sole demonstration of this fugue's three subjects in counterpoint with each other.

Anomalous for its great length and its lack of proper closure, this final fugue from Bach's pen nevertheless found champions in the late eighteenth and early nineteenth centuries. Sometime around 1800, the Austrian organist Joseph Diettenhofer played it and other fugues by Handel, Bach, and himself at the Savoy Church in London before a crowd of "several organists and eminent musicians," who in turn recommended publication. Lacking access to the manuscript sources, Diettenhofer simply tacked onto the 1751/52 reading (in his 1802 *Selection of Ten Miscellaneous Pieces*) a full cadence to D minor. Early nineteenth-century editions of the entire *Art of Fugue* likewise perpetuate the abridged reading with either a concluding half or full cadence. Only in 1878 were the missing bars restored, thanks to Wilhelm Rust's edition of the work for the Bach Gesellschaft.

Capitalizing on the insight Rust provided, Beethoven scholar Gustav Nottebohm demonstrated in 1881 that the unfinished fugue's three themes can also accommodate in invertible counterpoint the dotted variant of the main theme of the larger work. This turned Bach's final fugue into that rarest of contrapuntal beasts: a compound fugue with four subjects. Nottebohm's discovery prompted Tovey to find a few more combinations of all four themes, which he duly included in his 1931 edition of the *Art of Fugue*. Dozens of other completions have followed, many of which (like Tovey's) turn an already lengthy fugue into a veritable leviathan of counterpoint, with multiple rotating complexes of all themes displayed proudly in a new concluding section.

While Tovey was channeling Bach compositionally, the Germans were performing the *Art of Fugue*, mostly in Graeser's popular orchestration, which builds in the final fugue's B-A-C-H section to a tremendous climax that grows faint as the texture reduces to a single voice. Eyewitness accounts of early performances, collected in Eggebrecht's religiously infused monograph (1993) on the entire work, convey the reverential, hushed atmosphere of a solemn ritual. At the 1928 Kassel Bach Festival, as the last notes died away, the celestially gentle final chorale . . . entered to usher us into the realm of eternity. Audience members stood transfixed, while they listened to the pulsating sounds of painful sadness that hovered over them. There was no sound of applause. Only a foreboding sense of mysticism prevailed, which groped its way, in the shadow of death, after the secretive form of the dead master.

Performances without an interpolated ending still puzzle audiences, with the sudden silence making applause awkward if not impossible. Appending the chorale from the original edition, as the above report makes clear, encourages interpretation of this moment as a *memento mori*, a musical re-enactment of the beloved composer's death with a heartfelt prayer for his eternal rest.

Even Hofstadter—whose daffy actors camp it up in the other Bach-inspired vignettes in *Gödel, Escher, Bach*—highlights the uncanny side of this "failed" composition. His "Contracrostipunctus" episode has Tortoise explaining to Achilles as follows: "When I heard [this fugue] for the first time, I had no idea how it would end. Suddenly, without warning, it broke off . . . I realized immediately that was where Bach died." The B-A-C-H theme, in this darkly charming vignette, ruptures (through self-reference) Bach's own formal system, providing a handy illustration of logician Kurt Gödel's incompleteness theorem. The effect is sudden and jarring. As Tortoise plays the unfinished fugue's final notes, "without warning, a shattering sound rudely interrupts his performance. Both he and Achilles spin around, just in time to catch a glimpse of myriad fragments of glass tinkling to the floor from the shelf . . . and then . . . dead silence."

The path from fugal fissure to gothic apparition relies, ultimately, on the witness of Bach's son. But we know that Emanuel was not in Leipzig in the summer of 1750 as his father lay dying and, moreover, that the elder Bach's blindness rendered him incapable of composing in his own hand months before his death in July of that year. Also inarguable is what went missing, at least in broad outline. The standard explanation, as propounded by Wolff (1991b) and others, finds clues in the odd appearance of the final page of Bach's manuscript: sloppy ruling and the presence of a single (unused) staff between its first and second notated braces suggest that this was simply a useful scrap that provided a bridge from one thing to the next; the previous four pages are ruled precisely and have no randomly skipped staves. Wolff assumes, quite reasonably, that Bach began this fugue by sketching its conclusion, in which at least three and perhaps four subjects appear in multiple invertible complexes with each other. This would have been an obvious first step for Bach, who surely began any fugue with multiple subjects by tailoring each to allow for such combinations. Relying on probable compositional process, this optimistic theory dangles the enticing prospect of a "Fragment X" that Bach worked out first. Unfortunately, this veritable Rosetta Stone of invertible counterpoint with multiple themes either vanished at his death or was misunderstood by his heirs as part of an additional unrealized final fugue and was therefore laid aside. The latter summation fugue, according to the 1754 obituary authored by C. P. E. Bach and Agricola, "was to contain four themes and to have been afterward inverted note for note in all four voices."

Alternative accounts bracket the unfinished fugue as merely one of several capstone fugues that Bach planned for the work (Siegele 1988), as an experiment within the whole, analogous to the *Ricercar a 3* in *Musical Offering* (Dirksen 1994 and Wilson 2014), or as a separate piece entirely (Butler 2008). Of these, Butler's argument relies on the firmest evidence from the sources: small details in the engraver's copy of Contrapunctus 13 may identify it as the "next-to-last fugue" Bach intended for the work (the one the obituary claims lay unfinished at the composer's death), thereby orphaning the "Fuga a 3 Soggetti." This assumes that Bach never got around to writing a final mirror fugue in four parts, as the authors of his obituary suggest. Harder to swallow is the idea that such a piece could really accommodate four themes. Given the staggering compositional challenge of a quadruple mirror inversion fugue, Thomas Daniel (2018), among others, concludes that such a piece "would be pure illusion." Contrapuncti 12 and 13 offer useful reminders in this regard. Only the first is, properly speaking, a mirror fugue; the second (as noted in Chapter 4) is a rotating counter-fugue; both are, moreover, premised on a single subject. Daniel wonders, as we might, whether the authors of the obituary exaggerated Bach's capabilities or misunderstood his intentions.

Butler's proposal modifies his own earlier hypothesis (1983b) that Bach meant for the "Fuga a 3 Soggetti" to crown the series of fugues as Contrapunctus 14 and to incorporate four themes, a view that came to be widely shared. In a more recent essay (2008), Butler suggests instead that Bach composed it as an independent submission for Mizler's Society of the Musical Sciences. Glen Wilson's alternative proposal safeguards its place in the larger work but as a triple fugue, one that served as a late substitution for the planned four-part mirror fugue with four themes, which proved too taxing an assignment. Comparing the basic procedure of the "Fuga a 3 Soggetti" to a ricercar from Frescobaldi's *Fiori Musicali*, Wilson finds, in both the first and second themes of the former, traces of the main theme of the *Art of Fugue*, as do Zoltán Göncz (1991 and 1996/97) and others. This animating principle of the variation ricercar extends, as Wilson further observes, to the entire collection, whose component parts all manifest variants of the parent theme. Bach surely knew that a variation ricercar obliges no return of the original subject, hence the unfinished fugue has but three themes in this hypothesis.

We have, in short, multiple explanations for the existence and intended dimensions of this sphinx-like fugue, each propounded with plausible though hardly airtight argument. Absent a miraculous discovery, the debates over whether this gigantic fugal torso belongs in the *Art of Fugue* and whether it was intended to have a fourth subject may be declared draws.

Anyone contemplating a new final section would profit from Göncz's (1996/97) catalogue of the combinatorial possibilities of its three extant subjects, with or without the main theme of the larger work. Most published completions include multiple invertible complexes of all four themes in different keys, as happens in the other compound fugues in the *Art of Fugue*. Moroney's keyboard edition (1989), for example, offers on two staves a few combinations of all four subjects plus a continuation of the dramatic chromaticism of the B-A-C-H section. Curiously, both his and Helmut Walcha's more ambitious concluding section (in a 1967 edition for organ) ignore Tovey's demonstration of four-part complexes with the first subject transposed by a fifth or a twelfth, as Kevin Korsyn (2016) has pointed out. At just thirty bars, Moroney's otherwise skillful conclusion leaves this player wanting a bit more (a final pedal point, perhaps?) so that Bach's monumental fugue might close with commensurate grandeur. Behind Moroney's no-nonsense ending lurks Butler's (1983b) discovery of evolving page numbers during the engraving process, which left room for a missing section of approximately forty bars. But Butler's later (2008) change of heart about the piece itself, casting it out entirely from the larger work, may obviate this restriction.

The Italian composer Luciano Berio took a different tack in his 2001 transcription for chamber orchestra, entitled (following the order of the Bach Gesellschaft edition) *Contrapunctus XIX*. As Webern did in his orchestration of the *Ricercar a 6*, Berio mixes and matches instrumental timbres with great flair, creating a kaleidoscopic sound world for this even longer Bach fugue. But Berio also appends an enigmatic coda—not a properly contrapuntal completion, but rather a contemporary enclosure for the gradually disappearing texture of the autograph. A few dozen bars before the original breaks off, a quiet pedal D begins in the contrabass, to which more pitches are added in the other instruments, eventually forming a cluster. The resulting sonic haze envelops—in a warm if dissonant embrace—Bach's final notes, which linger in the memory as the delicate mass dissipates. The eerily beautiful ending, reminiscent of the slow fizzle of a failing television or computer monitor, provides respectful closure while avoiding the potential snares of new contrapuntal invention.

That such a strategy should have occurred to Berio, perhaps the least doctrinaire of the postwar avant-garde, is not surprising, given his longstanding interest in older music and his commitment to compositional lost causes. His subsequent (2002) completion of *Turandot* likewise honors what Puccini left behind, including sketches for the problematic final scene, without trying to channel somehow the muse of the deceased composer. Of course, an incomplete stage work often requires more than just a framing device, even if this means welcoming a new compositional voice as co-creator. The same holds true for unfinished sacred and orchestral works. Major intervention has been the rule for many a fragmentary musical work over the years, and for good reason: without such efforts, the Mozart *Requiem* would be unperformable. Moreover, when we leave an artwork incomplete, we "endow it with an intrigue that lends the work a contradictory identity," as Pierre-Michel Menger (2010) cautions. *Faute de mieux*, Bach's unfinished fugue continues to be included in editions and performances of the work with which it has been associated since 1751, sometimes exactly as Bach left it and sometimes with additional material. Anyone presenting this piece in an edition or in concert is obliged, in other words, to embrace the silence or to fill it somehow. Berio's ethereally static conclusion, characteristically, brushes aside more traditional efforts as somehow beside the point.

I say this not to diminish the achievement of those who labor to channel Bach but rather to situate their efforts within the curiously bifurcated reception history of his unfinished fugue. The belief that Bach died while at work on it has encouraged many to regard its disintegration (and, by association, that of the larger work) as a moment of spiritual transfiguration. Alongside this interpretive trope arose a practical response, one rooted in diligent study of eighteenth-century counterpoint and of Bach's habits especially, whose goal is the best possible ending to an uncommonly ambitious fugue. Those who take up the latter challenge, I would argue, enter more fully into the spirit of the work itself and the milieu that produced it.

Differently said, the value we assign to incomplete though authentic texts can encourage an unhelpfully dogmatic attitude toward the surviving portion, a fetishization of the extant text over its completion. Interestingly, this tendency manifested itself in the late 1920s and 1930s in the difficult gestation of other unfinished major works, just as orchestrations of the *Art of Fugue* (in its canonic form with the prayerful pause and the chorale postlude) found a grateful public for Bach's final fugal corpus. At the premiere of *Turandot* in 1926, Arturo Toscanini brought Puccini's last opera to a sudden stop at the very moment where the composer died, as the conductor announced to its opening night audience. Franco Alfano's much-maligned conclusion, which had been commissioned by Puccini's publisher, was heard only at subsequent performances, after Toscanini had made his point. A similar reluctance to consent to the inevitable can be found in the complicated performance history of Alban Berg's *Lulu* (1935), whose final act lay incomplete at the composer's death. Once Schoenberg, Webern, and Alexander von Zemlinsky all rejected entreaties from Universal Edition to flesh out Berg's sketches for the closing scenes, the composer's widow prevented the opera's completion for decades.

The manifold mechanical tasks involved in salvaging an unfinished musical torso are compounded by the medium itself: incompleteness in the performing arts, as Menger and others remind us, is a more difficult problem than incompleteness in visual art or literature. Music's formal density and abstract nature render the completion of an abandoned musical work a particularly fraught enterprise. A surviving libretto or text might provide essential information to a surrogate composer, but an unfinished instrumental work—particularly one shaped by a mix of fugal procedures and free counterpoint rather than a conventional formal scheme—provides few guideposts for completion. Most who have tried to complete Bach's unfinished fugue therefore acknowledge only the most obvious parameters: namely, that this is a compound fugue on multiple subjects, each of which is explored individually before being combined with the others, and that all themes ought to appear in a closing section, preferably in rotating invertible complexes deployed in various keys, including the tonic. In the final bars he committed to paper, Bach began this process with a single combination of the three subjects introduced thus far. What happens next is for us to decide.

Drawing on the work of Nottebohm, Tovey, and others, we might regard the missing ending as a daunting though by no means impossible assignment: a comprehensive exam, as it were, on the fugal art. This kind of thinking is not without historical justification. Users of the original open-score edition would likely have transcribed onto two staves other portions of the *Art of Fugue* before arriving at the "Fuga a 3 Soggetti," so pen and paper would already have been dedicated to such work. Numerous unrealized canons, which Bach expected contemporaries to solve on their own, can be found in his engraved prints from just a few years before, including three of five *Vom Himmel hoch* canons and nine of ten canons in *Musical Offering*, some of which admit multiple solutions. Canon, of course, typically requires no compositional "filler"; one deduces from clues left by the composer or copyist how an unnotated but authorized voice fits into an imposed texture. The last seven measures of Bach's unfinished fugue may constitute an analogous prompt for a more challenging task: crafting a suitable ending from the given complex of three themes and other potential combinations. But with precisely those measures suppressed in the first edition of the *Art of Fugue*, Bach's posthumous editors ensured that their contemporaries would not solve this musical puzzle. Perhaps one or more of his heirs wanted first crack at it.

Anyone who engages seriously with this work will eventually ponder what might have been, with the bravest trying to fill that void with as much art as possible. That much we have in common with musicians of Bach's era, for whom an unfinished fugue would have constituted an incongruous ending for an elaborate series of written-out fugues and canons. Incomplete notation of canon had long been standard in manuscript and printed sources, but incomplete fugues in the eighteenth century were the stuff of compositional notebooks, not expensive engraved editions. To be appreciated properly, either kind of piece needed (and still needs) to be resolved.

And yet, we diverge radically from Bach and his brethren in our modern reverence for the whole, thanks to an evolving concept of the musical work and our institutionalized preservation of the music of past ages. With scholarly and performing editions that reflect longstanding obsessions with correct order and contents, we privilege our culture's aesthetic priorities and habits of consumption. It's hard to imagine even the most fanatical of eighteenth-century disciples playing the entirety of the *Art of Fugue*, *Musical Offering*, or either book of the *WTC* in front of an audience, as we commonly do; nor did works like the "Brandenburg" Concertos or Bach's *Christmas Oratorio* then constitute integral wholes. I point this out not to discourage performances, recordings, or comprehensive studies of any of these works, but rather to emphasize how much the musical world has changed over the last three hundred years and how profoundly that shift has affected the reception of such music.

The dominance of "complete" musical works in our world prompts a few closing thoughts on how best to experience these masterpieces of late Baroque counterpoint. Surviving exemplars of the first edition of *Musical Offering*, few of which include all five printing sections, suggest that it functioned for Bach's contemporaries as a repository of related pieces, not an inviolable entity. Even Bach's staunchest defenders felt no obligation toward the entire work: in a 1752 letter to another member of his society, Mizler describes this royal gift as comprising just "three pieces—a trio, a ricercar, and a fugue." That aspect of reception has hardly changed; Bach's *Musical Offering* remains a compositional grab bag that cuts across genres and instruments, with the original and subsequent editions imposing neither a definitive order on its contents nor an obligation for performance of the whole. The sonata, now a cornerstone of the Baroque trio repertoire, is the most frequently heard item, with the ricercari played regularly on keyboard instruments and in various transcriptions. The ten canons are perhaps best sampled individually, as one does with a box of exquisite chocolates, and in the company of musically proficient friends.

For an initial encounter with either collection, a "whole-hog" approach may not be the wisest strategy. An old German pun warns of the dangers of listening to or playing the entire *Art of Fugue* in one sitting: too much *d-moll* (D minor) leaves one *demolliert* or "demolished." There is some truth in this, although the manifold challenges of ascending this Parnassus of the fugal style while savoring every step and switchback will always appeal to some. The experience can be invigorating on multiple levels, with the requisite stamina and reserves acquired in stages. Player and listener alike stand to benefit by focusing first on basic elements of compositional craft and organization: procedures like invertible counterpoint, or the order of items in a group of pieces. From there one progresses to more complex issues such as the subtle distinctions between subgenres of fugue or the implications of Latin rubrics in canon. In addition to a deeper understanding of Bach's music, such expertise may provide occasional insights in other disciplines, from painting to physics.

The seemingly more straightforward matter of instrumentation relies, ultimately, on the ongoing negotiation between tactile or acoustic preferences and respect for historical conventions.

Few works of Bach (or any other composer, for that matter) have been transcribed more often and for such wildly diverse forces. Harpsichord, as its modern champions insist, was indeed the most logical vehicle in Bach's day for the *Art of Fugue*, but that hardly forbids other possibilities. The same may be said for the two ricercari and most of the canons in *Musical Offering*, which Bach left similarly unassigned though in notational formats then common for keyboard music. He did this for good reason: a sensitive performance of a Bach fugue or canon by a single player can focus the mind and ear on its many subtleties. That said, a thoughtful chamber reading might expand the conversation with a variety of timbres. Recorded and live performances of the *Art of Fugue* and *Musical Offering* offer myriad ways to appreciate this sturdy music as realized by viol consorts, saxophone quartets, jazz vocalists, or solo keyboardists, among other options. Each colors the counterpoint differently, with the finest efforts infusing Bach's deeply learned art with spontaneity, wit, and feeling.

For some scholars the exceptional nature of these works frees them somehow from the here and now. In their respective praise for Webern's orchestration of the *Ricercar a 6* (referenced in Chapter 5), for example, both Adorno and Dahlhaus maintain that this fugue transcends the limitations of instruments. Given its frequently intertwined lines, even experienced harpsichordists may agree with this assessment. But Dahlhaus goes further, asserting that "a truly satisfactory instrumental presentation of the ricercar is located in the no-man's land between what was not yet possible in Bach's time and what is no longer possible in our own." Though an attractive notion, this pushes the envelope too far, I think, beyond actual music-making into the unknowable realm of *musica speculativa*, with no apparent gain to our appreciation of Bach's (or Webern's) ideas. The notion of an ideal performance, moreover, would have found little resonance among Bach or his peers, who had multiple reasons for composing and contemplating learned contrapuntal works intended primarily for private edification and enjoyment.

Unsurprisingly, Dahlhaus's attempt to park Webern's transcription in a philosophical cul-de-sac has had little discernable effect: the orchestrated *Fuga a 6* still enjoys considerable popularity. And why not? Its constantly mutating colors, combined with copious dynamic and articulation markings, yield a remarkably transparent orchestral fugue.

Ultimately, the notion that any musical work can inhabit a kind of existential waiting room, where it may be perfected by some future creative genius or ensemble, delegitimizes historical practice while positing an agency that the notes themselves lack. As Bach himself demonstrated in both projects, practitioners decide for themselves what constitutes perfection. And that may change from one day to the next, as we continue to play and learn.

## SUGGESTIONS FOR FURTHER READING

In addition to a plethora of scholarly writing on Bach's unfinished fugue, some of which is cited above, there is lively literature devoted to the more general problem of incompleteness in artworks. See, for example, Pierre-Michel Menger, "Le travail à l'oeuvre: Enquête sur l'autorité contingente du créateur dans l'art lyrique" (2010); Richard Kramer, *Unfinished Music* (2008); or Robert Winter, "On Realizations, Completions, Restorations, and Reconstructions: From Bach's *The Art of Fugue* to Beethoven's Tenth Symphony" (1991).

# Glossary

**Appoggiatura:** a melodic figure comprising two adjacent notes, the first of which leans into the second, thus resolving an accented dissonance. Derived from the Italian verb *appoggiare*, which means "to lean."

**Augmentation:** the lengthening (generally by doubling) of all note values in a melody or fugue subject, so that it moves twice as slow as before.

**Cadence:** a simple harmonic formula that signals closure or resolution. Akin to a period in grammar, it affirms the central key of a discrete section or an entire piece.

**Canon:** a procedure in which a melody is repeated against itself (note for note) at staggered intervals of time. A canon may also incorporate complementary voices that do not imitate the canonic melody.

**Cantus firmus:** literally, a "fixed song" (Lat.), one delivered in longer notes than the surrounding counterpoint of a mass movement, chorale prelude, or other kind of piece. During the Renaissance and Baroque eras, these melodies were often borrowed from familiar chants or chorales.

**Circle of fifths:** a tool for describing and executing chord progressions by ascending or descending fifth. The resulting series of functionally related harmonies allows for tonic and dominant functions for each of the twelve chromatic pitches and is often depicted by a circle summarizing those relationships.

**Continuo** (*basso continuo*): the Baroque practice of realizing a bass line and numerical figures (whether indicated or implied) that specify intervals or chords above that bass.

**Counterpoint:** two or more interdependent musical lines in a shared texture. Unlike melody-dominated music, counterpoint mandates certain manners of voice leading between the parts, whose totality produces harmony.

**Diminution:** the shortening (generally by half) of all note values in a melody or fugue subject, so that it moves twice as fast as before.

**Fair copy**: a clean hand copy of a work, which may incorporate revisions to earlier versions of the same piece. In Bach's day a fair copy commonly served for either performance or as a reference for additional copies or a published edition.

**False (cross) relation**: a pungent dissonance that juxtaposes a single diatonic note against its chromatic neighbor (e.g., F♮ against F♯).

**Fugue**: a procedure premised on a melody or "subject" that is developed imitatively, with staggered entries initially in all the parts and reappearances of that melody in various guises as the fugue runs its course.

**Galant**: a style that emphasizes elegance and ease, common to mid-eighteenth-century literature, art, and music.

**Imitation**: the repetition in multiple voices of a short motive or melody at varying intervals of time.

**Inversion (melodic)**: turning a melody upside down to make all its intervals move in the opposite direction, creating a mirror image of the original.

**Invertible counterpoint**: inverting the registral relationships of two or more independent lines. In a piece of two-part counterpoint, this procedure moves the top voice to the bottom of the texture, and vice versa.

**Ostinato**: a continually repeating melodic or rhythmic pattern.

**Retrograde**: reordering of a melody or fugue subject so that it is delivered with all its pitches and rhythms in reverse, from back to front.

**Ricercar**: literally, a piece that "searches out" or "seeks" (der. from the Italian verb *ricercare*). During the Baroque era, the term was applied to improvisatory pieces as well as rigorously contrapuntal works that are often sectional in nature.

**Sequence**: a series of repeating motives or harmonic patterns at multiple pitch levels.

**Stile antico**: the "ancient style" of sixteenth-century counterpoint, as taught and practiced by generations of musicians since that time.

**Transposition**: shifting a discrete passage, section, or an entire piece up or down in pitch, thus changing its key.

# Select Bibliography

## Editions

### The Art of Fugue

Kunst der Fuge/Art of Fugue BWV 1080, edited by Peter Williams. London and Mainz: Eulenburg, 1986.

Die Kunst der Fuge/The Art of Fugue BWV 1080, edited by Christoph Wolff. Frankfurt and New York: C. F. Peters, 1987.

Die Kunst der Fuge, edited by Davitt Moroney. Munich: Henle, 1989.

Die Kunst der Fuge/The Art of Fugue, edited by Klaus Hofmann. Kassel: Bärenreiter, 1998.

"The Art of the Fugue," edited by José Rodriguez Alvira. téoria: Music Theory Web. https://www.teoria.com/en/articles/kdf/.

NB The autograph materials and the original 1751/52 engraved print, as well as multiple other editions, are available electronically through the International Music Score Library Project: https://imslp.org/wiki/Die_Kunst_der_Fuge,_BWV_1080_(Bach,_Johann_Sebastian).

### Musical Offering

Musikalisches Opfer/Musical Offering BWV 1079, edited by Peter Williams. London and Mainz: Eulenburg, 1986.

A Musical Offering, edited by Christoph Wolff. Kassel: Bärenreiter, 1987/88.

NB Multiple editions, including the original 1747 engraved print, are available electronically through the International Music Score Library Project: https://imslp.org/wiki/Musikalisches_Opfer%2C_BWV_1079_(Bach%2C_Johann_Sebastian).

## Literature

Adorno, Theodor. "Bach Defended against his Devotees." In Prisms, translated by Samuel and Shierry Weber, 133–146. Cambridge, MA: MIT Press, 1982 (orig. 1951).

Benjamin, Thomas. The Craft of Tonal Counterpoint. New York: Routledge, 2003.

Bullivant, Roger. Fugue. London: Hutchinson & Co, 1971.

Butler, Gregory G. "*Der vollkommene Capellmeister* as a Stimulus to J. S. Bach's Late Fugal Writing." In *New Mattheson Studies*, edited by George J. Buelow and Hans Joachim Marx, 293–305. Cambridge: Cambridge University Press, 1983 [1983a].

Butler, Gregory G. "Ordering Problems in J. S. Bach's *Art of Fugue* Resolved." *Musical Quarterly* 69, no. 1 (Winter 1983): 44–61 [1983b].

Butler, Gregory G. "The Printing History of J. S. Bach's Musical Offering: New Interpretations." *Journal of Musicology* 19, no. 2 (Spring 2002): 306–331 [2002a].

Butler, Gregory G. "The 'Galant' Style in J. S. Bach's *Musical Offering*: Widening the Dimensions." *BACH* 33, no. 1 (2002): 57–68 [2002b].

Butler, Gregory G. "Scribes, Engravers, and Notational Styles: The Final Disposition of Bach's Art of Fugue." In *About Bach*, edited by Gregory G. Butler, George B. Stauffer, and Mary Dalton Greer, 111–124. Urbana and Chicago: University of Illinois Press, 2008.

Chafe, Eric. "Allegorical Music: The 'Symbolism' of Tonal Language in the Bach Canons." *Journal of Musicology* 3, no. 4 (Autumn 1984): 340–362.

Chapin, Keith. "Scheibe's Mistake: Sublime Simplicity and the Criteria of Classicism." *18th-Century Music* 5 (2008): 165–177.

Chapin, Keith. "Bach's Silence, Mattheson's Words: Professional and Humanist Ways of Speaking of Music." In *Speaking of Music: Addressing the Sonorous*, edited by Keith Chapin and Andrew H. Clark, 49–69. New York: Fordham University Press, 2013.

Collins, Denis. "Bach and Approaches to Canonic Composition in Early Eighteenth-Century Theoretical and Chamber Music Sources." *BACH* 30, no. 2 (1999): 27–48.

Collins, Denis. "From Bull to Bach: In Search of Precedents for the 'Complete' Version of the Canon by Augmentation and Contrary Motion in J. S. Bach's Musical Offering." *BACH* 37, no. 2 (2007): 39–63.

Collins, Denis, and Andrew Schloss. "An Unusual Effect in the Canon per Tonos from J. S. Bach's Musical Offering." *Music Perception: An Interdisciplinary Journal* 19 (2001): 141–153.

Dahlhaus, Carl. "Bach's Six-Part Ricercar as Orchestrated by Anton Webern." In *Schoenberg and the New Music*, translated by Derrick Puffett and Alfred Clayton, 181–191. Cambridge: Cambridge University Press, 1987.

Daniel, Thomas. "War Bachs letzte Fuge als Quadrupel-Spiegelfuge konzipiert?" *Bach Jahrbuch* 104 (2018): 113–132.

Daub, Peggy. "The Publication Process and Audience for C. P. E. Bach's *Sonaten für Kenner und Liebhaber*." In *Bach Perspectives 2: J. S. Bach, the Breitkopfs, and Eighteenth-Century Music Trade*, edited by George B. Stauffer, 65–82. Lincoln: University of Nebraska Press, 1996.

David, Hans T. *J. S. Bach's Musical Offering*. New York: Schirmer, 1945; New York: Dover, 1972.

David, Hans T. "The Art of the Fugue." *BACH* 1, no. 3 (1970): 5–21.

Demeyere, Ewald. *Johann Sebastian Bach's Art of Fugue: Performance Practice Based on German Eighteenth-Century Theory.* Leuven: Leuven University Press, 2013.

Dentler, Hans-Eberhard. *Johann Sebastian Bachs "Kunst der Fuge": Ein pythagoreisches Werk und seine Verwirklichung.* Mainz: Schott, 2004.

Dentler, Hans-Eberhard. *Johann Sebastian Bachs "Musicalisches Opfer": Musik als Abbild der Sphärenharmonie.* Berlin: Schott, 2008.

Dickinson, Alan Edgar Frederic. *Bach's Fugal Works: With an Account of Fugue Before and After Bach.* London: Pitman & Sons, 1956; Westport, CT: Greenwood Press, 1979.

Dirksen, Pieter. *Studien zur Kunst der Fuge von Joh. Seb. Bach.* Veröfferntlichungen zur Musikforschung 12. Wilhelmshaven: Florian Noetzel Verlag, 1994.

Dirst, Matthew. *Engaging Bach: The Keyboard Legacy from Marpurg to Mendelssohn.* Cambridge: Cambridge University Press, 2012.

Dreyfus, Laurence. *Bach and the Patterns of Invention.* Cambridge, MA: Harvard University Press, 1996.

Edwards, Timothy D. "The Royal Theme's Hidden Symmetry: In Defense of the Concise Solution to the Augmentation Canon in J. S. Bach's 'Musical Offering'." *BACH* 41, no. 1 (2010): 1–31.

Eggebrecht, Hans Heinrich. *Kunst der Fuge: Erscheinung und Deutung.* Munich: Piper, 1984. Republished as *J. S. Bach's The Art of Fugue.* Translated by Jeffrey L. Prater. Ames, IA: Iowa State University Press, 1993.

Ferris, David. "Plates for Sale: C. P. E. Bach and the Story of *Die Kunst der Fuge*." In *C. P. E. Bach Studies*, edited by Annette Richards, 202–220. Cambridge: Cambridge University Press, 2006.

Forkel, Johann Nikolaus. "On Johann Sebastian Bach's Life, Genius, and Works." In *The New Bach Reader: A Life of Johann Sebastian Bach in Letters and Documents*, edited by Hans T. David and Arthur Mendel, revised by Christoph Wolff, 417–482. New York: Norton, 1998.

Fux, Johann Joseph. *Gradus ad Parnassum.* Vienna, 1725. Partially translated in Alfred Mann, *The Study of Fugue* (New York: Norton, 1965).

Gaines, James. *Evening in the Palace of Reason.* London: Harper Perennial, 2005.

Gauldin, Robert. *A Practical Approach to 18th-Century Counterpoint.* Long Grove, IL: Waveland Press, 2013.

Göncz, Zoltán. "The Permutational Matrix in J. S. Bach's Art of Fugue. The Last Fugue Finished?" *Studia Musicologica Academiae Scientiarum Hungaricae* 33, nos. 1–4 (1991): 109–119.

Göncz, Zoltán. "Reconstruction of the Final Contrapunctus of *The Art of Fugue*." *International Journal of Musicology* 5 (1996): 25–93 and 6 (1997): 103–119.

Göncz, Zoltán. "The Sacred Codes of the Six-Part Ricercar." *BACH* 42, no. 1 (2011): 46–69.

Göncz, Zoltán. *Bach's Testament: On the Philosophical and Theological Background of The Art of Fugue.* Lanham, MD: The Scarecrow Press, 2013.

Greenberg, Yoel. "'Ordo AB Chao': The Fugue as Chaos in the Early Twentieth Century." *Music & Letters* 99, no. 1 (February 2018): 74–103.

HaCohen, Ruth. "The Tonal, the Gestural, and the Allegorical in Bach's *Musical Offering.*" *Understanding Bach* 1 (2006): 19–38.

Harriss, Ernst Charles. *Johann Mattheson's Der vollkommene Capellmeister: A Revised Translation with Critical Commentary.* Ann Arbor, MI: UMI Research Press, 1981.

Hofstadter, Douglas R. *Gödel, Escher, Bach: An Eternal Golden Braid.* New York: Basic Books, 1979.

Hoke, Hans Gunter. "Neue Studien zur Kunst der Fuge, BWV 1080." *Beiträge zur Muskwissenschaft* 17, nos. 2–3 (1975): 95–115.

Husmann, Heinrich. "Die Kunst der Fuge als Klavierwerk." *Bach-Jahrbuch* 35 (1938): 1–61.

Kennan, Kent. *Counterpoint: Based on Eighteenth-Century Practice,* 4th edition. Upper Saddle River, NJ: Prentice-Hall, 1999.

Kerman, Joseph. *The Art of Fugue: Bach's Fugues for Keyboard 1715–1750.* Berkeley: University of California Press, 2005.

Kirkendale, Ursula. "The Source for Bach's *Musical Offering:* The *Institutio oratoria* of Quintilian." *Journal of the American Musicological Society* 33 (1980): 88–141.

Kirkendale, Warren. *Fugue and Fugato in Rococo and Classical Chamber Music.* Durham, NC: Duke University Press, 1979 [1979a].

Kirkendale, Warren. "Ciceronians versus Aristotelians on the Ricercar as Exordium from Bembo to Bach." *Journal of the American Musicological Society* 32 (1979): 1–44 [1979b].

Kirkendale, Warren. "On the Rhetorical Interpretation of the Ricercar and J. S. Bach's *Musical Offering.*" *Studi Musicali* 26 (1997): 331–371.

Kistler-Liebendörfer, Bernhard. *Quaerendo invenietis: Versuch über J. S. Bachs Musikalisches Opfer.* Frankfurt: Fischer, 1985.

Klee, Paul. *Notebooks, Volume 1: The Thinking Eye.* Translated by Charlotte Weidler and Joyce Wittenborn. London: Lund Humphries, 1961.

Kolneder, Walter. *Die Kunst der Fuge.* Wilhelmshaven, 1977.

Korsyn, Kevin. "At the Margins of Music Theory, History, and Composition: Completing the Unfinished Fugue in *Die Kunst der Fuge* by J. S. Bach." *Music Theory & Analysis* 3, no. 11 (October 2016): 115–143.

Kramer, Richard. *Unfinished Music.* Oxford and New York: Oxford University Press, 2008.

Leonhardt, Gustav M. *The Art of Fugue, Bach's Last Harpsichord Work: An Argument.* The Hague: Martinus Nijhoff, 1952.

MacDonough, Giles. *Frederick the Great: A Life in Deed and Letters*. New York: St. Martin's Press, 1999.

Mann, Alfred. *The Study of Fugue*. New York: Dover, 1987.

Marissen, Michael. "More Source-Critical Research on Bach's *Musical Offering*." *BACH* 25 (1994): 11–27.

Marissen, Michael. "The Theological Character of J. S. Bach's *Musical Offering*." In *Bach Studies* 2, edited by Daniel R. Melamed, 85–106. Cambridge: Cambridge University Press, 1995.

Markham, Michael. "'The Usefulness of Such Artworks': Expression, Analysis, and Nationalism in *The Art of Fugue*." *Repercussions* 9 (2001): 33–75.

Marpurg, Friedrich Wilhelm. *Abhandlung von der Fuge*. Berlin, 1753; Hildesheim: Georg Olms Verlag, 2013. Partially translated in Alfred Mann, *The Study of Fugue* (New York: Norton, 1965).

Menger, Pierre-Michel. "Le travail à l'oeuvre: Enquête sur l'autorité contingente du créateur dans l'art lyrique." *Annales. Historie, Sciences Sociales* 65, no. 3 (May-June 2010): 743–786.

Milka, Anatoly. "*Quaerendo invenietis* in J. S. Bach's *Musical Offering* BWV 1079*." *Israel Studies in Musicology Online* 13 (2015/16): 46–50.

Milka, Anatoly. *Rethinking J. S. Bach's The Art of Fugue*. Translated by Maria Ritzarev and edited by Esti Sheinberg. New York: Routledge, 2017.

Niedt, Friedrich Erhardt. *The Musical Guide: Parts 1–3 (1710–1721)*, translated by Pamela L. Poulin and Irmgard C. Taylor. Oxford: Clarendon Press, 1989.

Oleskiewicz, Mary. "The Trio in Bach's Musical Offering: A Salute to Frederick's Tastes and Quantz's Flutes?" In *Bach Perspectives 4: The Music of J. S. Bach—Analysis and Interpretation*, edited by David Schulenberg, 79–110. Lincoln: University of Nebraska Press, 1999.

Oleskiewicz, Mary. "Keyboards, Music Rooms, and the Bach Family at the Court of Frederick the Great." In *Bach Perspectives 11: J. S. Bach and His Sons*, edited by Mary Oleskiewicz, 24–82. Urbana: University of Illinois Press, 2017.

Op de Coul, Thomas. "The Augmentation Canon in J. S. Bach's *Musicalisches Opfer*." *BACH* 37, no. 1 (2006): 50–77.

Parker, Roger. *Remaking the Song: Operatic Visions and Revisions from Handel to Berio*. Berkeley: University of California Press, 2006.

Parks, Richard S. *Eighteenth-Century Counterpoint and Tonal Structure*. Englewood Cliffs, NJ: Prentice-Hall, 1984.

Rampe, Siegbert. "Bach, Quantz und das 'Musicalische Opfer'." *Concerto: Das Magazin für Alte Musik* 10, no. 84 (1993): 15–23.

Rivera, Benito V. "Bach's Use of Hitherto Unrecognized Types of Countersubjects in the 'Art of Fugue.'" *Journal of the American Musicological Society* 31 (1978): 344–362.

Scheibe, Johann Adolph. *Critischer Musikus*, 2nd edition. Leipzig, 1745; Hildesheim: G. Olms, 1970.

Schieckel, Harald. "Johann Sebastian Bachs Auflösung eines Kanons von Teodoro Riccio." *Bach-Jahrbuch* 68 (1982): 125–130.

Schleuning, Peter. *Johann Sebastian Bachs "Kunst der Fuge": Ideologien—Entstehung—Analyse.* Kassel: Bärenreiter, 1993.

Schubert, Peter, and Christopher Neidhöfer. *Baroque Counterpoint.* Upper Saddle River, NJ: Pearson Prentice Hall, 2006.

Schulenberg, David. *The Keyboard Music of J. S. Bach*, 2nd edition. New York: Routledge, 2006.

Sheveloff, Joel. *J. S. Bach's Musical Offering: An Eighteenth-Century Conundrum.* Lewiston, NY: Edwin Mellen Press, 2013.

Siegele, Ulrich. "Wie unvollständig ist Bachs Kunst der Fuge?" In *Johann Sebastian Bach: Weltbild, Menschenbild, Notenbild, Klangbild*, edited by Winfried Hoffmann and Armin Schneiderheinze, 219–225. Leipzig: VEB Deutscher Verlag für Musik, 1988.

Siegele, Ulrich. "Technik des Komponisten vor der Größe des Herrschers: Das dreistimmige Ricercar aus dem Musikalischen Opfer von J. S. Bach." In *Musik als Klangreded: Festschrift zum 70. Geburtstag von Günter Fleischhauer*, edited by Wolfgang Ruf, 156–193. Cologne: Böhlau, 2001.

Spitta, Philipp. *Johann Sebastian Bach.* Leipzig, 1873/80. Translated by Clara Bell and J. A. Fuller-Maitland as *The Life of Bach.* London: Novello, 1884–89.

Stauffer, George B. "Johann Mattheson and J. S. Bach: The Hamburg Connection." In *New Mattheson Studies*, edited by George J. Buelow and Hans Joachim Marx, 353–368. Cambridge: Cambridge University Press, 1983.

Talle, Andrew. "A Print of *Clavierübung* I from J. S. Bach's Personal Library." In *About Bach*, edited by Gregory G. Butler, George B. Stauffer, and Mary Dalton Greer, 157–168. Urbana and Chicago: University of Illinois Press, 2008.

Talle, Andrew. *Beyond Bach: Music and Everyday Life in the Eighteenth Century.* Urbana: University of Illinois Press, 2017.

Thormählen, Wiebke. "Playing with Art: Musical Arrangements as Educational Tools in van Swieten's Vienna." *The Journal of Musicology* 27, no. 3 (Summer 2010): 342–376.

Tovey, Donald Francis. *A Companion to 'The Art of Fugue'.* London: Oxford University Press, 1931.

Trythall, H. Gilbert. *Eighteenth-Century Counterpoint.* Madison, WI: Brown & Benchmark, 1992.

Verdi, Richard. "Musical Influences on the Art of Paul Klee." *Art Institute of Chicago Museum Studies* 3 (1968): 81–107.

Vergo, Peter. *The Music of Painting.* London: Phaidon Press, 2010.

Vogt, Hans. *Johann Sebastian Bachs Kammermusik.* Stuttgart: Philipp Reclam, 1981. Translated by Kenn Johnson as *Johann Sebastian Bach's Chamber*

*Music: Background, Analyses, Individual Works* (Portland, OR: Amadeus Press, 1988).

Walker, Paul Mark. "Rhetoric, the Ricercar, and J. S. Bach's *Musical Offering*." In *Bach Studies* 2, edited by Daniel R. Melamed, 175–191. Cambridge: Cambridge University Press, 1995.

Walker, Paul Mark. *Theories of Fugue from the Age of Josquin to the Age of Bach.* Rochester, NY: University of Rochester Press, 2000.

Walker, Paul Mark. "Counterpoint, Canon and the Late Works." In *The Routledge Research Companion to Johann Sebastian Bach*, edited by Robin A. Leaver, 377–397. London and New York: Routledge, 2017.

Walther, Johann Gottfried. *Praecepta der musicalischen Composition*, edited by Peter Benary. Leipzig: Breitkopf & Härtel, 1955 (orig. 1708).

Wiemer, Wolfgang. *Die widerhergestellte Ordnung in Johann Sebastian Bachs Kunst der Fuge. Untersuchungen am Original-Druck.* Wiesbaden: Breitkopf und Härtel, 1977.

Wilson, Glen. "Bach's Art of Fugue: Suggestions for the Last Gap." *Early Music* 42, no. 2 (2014): 249–257.

Williams, Peter. *J. S. Bach: A Life in Music.* Cambridge: Cambridge University Press, 2007.

Williams, Peter. "Frescobaldi's *Fiori musicali* and Bach." *Recercare* 24, nos. 1–2 (2012): 93–105.

Winter, Robert S. "On Realizations, Completions, Restorations, and Reconstructions: From Bach's *The Art of Fugue* to Beethoven's Tenth Symphony." *Journal of the Royal Musical Association* 116, no. 1 (1991): 96–126.

Wolff, Christoph. "Apropos the *Musical Offering*: The Thema Regium and the Term *Ricercar*." In *Bach: Essays on His Life and Music*, 324–331. Cambridge, MA: Harvard University Press, 1991 [1991a].

Wolff, Christoph. "Bach's Last Fugue: Unfinished?" In *Bach: Essays*, 259–264 [1991b].

Wolff, Christoph. "The Compositional History of the Art of Fugue." In *Bach: Essays*, 265–281 [1991c].

Wolff, Christoph. "The Deathbed Chorale: Exposing a Myth." In *Bach: Essays*, 282–294 [1991d].

Wolff, Christoph. "Design and Order in Bach's Original Editions." In *Bach: Essays*, 340–358 [1991e].

Wolff, Christoph. "New Research on the Musical Offering." In *Bach: Essays*, 239–258 [1991f].

Wolff, Christoph. *J. S. Bach: The Learned Musician.* New York: W. W. Norton, 2000.

Wolff, Christoph, and Hans T. David and Arthur Mendel, eds. *The New Bach Reader: A Life of Johann Sebastian Bach in Letters and Documents.* New York: Norton, 1998.

Yearsley, David. "The Alchemy of Bach's Canons." In *Bach and the Meanings of Counterpoint*, 42–92. Cambridge: Cambridge University Press, 2002 [2002a].

Yearsley, David. "The Autocratic Regimes of *A Musical Offering*." In *Bach and the Meanings of Counterpoint*, 128–172 [2002b].

Yearsley, David. "Bach the Machine." In *Bach and the Meanings of Counterpoint*, 173–208 [2002c].

Yearsley, David. "*Vor deinen Thron tret ich* and the Art of Dying." In *Bach and the Meanings of Counterpoint*, 1–41 [2002d].

Yearsley, David. "C. P. E. Bach and the Living Traditions of Learned Counterpoint." In *C. P. E. Bach Studies*, edited by Annette Richards, 173–201. Cambridge: Cambridge University Press, 2006.

# Index

*For the benefit of digital users, indexed terms that span two pages (e.g., 52–53) may, on occasion, appear on only one of those pages.*

Tables are indicated by *t* following the page number